Vermont

HILLSIDE ACRES

Vermont

Ann Heinrichs

Children's Press®
A Division of Grolier Publishing
New York   London   Hong Kong   Sydney
Danbury, Connecticut

Frontispiece: Aerial view of sumac in the autumn

Front cover: Fall foliage on a farm near Woodstock

Back cover: A covered bridge in Stowe

Consultant: Michael Sherman, Associate Professor, Vermont College of Norwich University

Please note: All statistics are as up-to-date as possible at the time of publication.

Visit Children's Press on the Internet at http://publishing.grolier.com

Book production by Editorial Directions, Inc.

Library of Congress Cataloging-in-Publication Data

Heinrichs, Ann.
   Vermont / by Ann Heinrichs.
      p. cm.—(America the beautiful. Second series)
   Includes bibliographic references and index.
   Summary : Describes the geography, plants and animals, history, economy, language, religions, culture and people of the state of Vermont.
   ISBN 0-516-21094-7
   1. Vermont—Juvenile literature. [1. Vermont.] I. Title. II. Series.
F49.3 .H45 2001
974.3—dc21   00-029480
                                                       CIP
                                                        AC

Acknowledgments

For their kind assistance in this project, I am grateful to innumerable employees of Vermont's tourism and agriculture departments, to the Vermont Division of Historic Preservation, and to all the Vermonters who shared their hospitality and experiences with me.

Rural Vermont

Small-town Vermont

Snowboarding at Sugarbush

Contents

Hermit thrush

Canoeing in Vermont

Lake Champlain

A young Vermonter

Grossular garnet

CHAPTER ONE

A Living Past

Tapping maple trees to collect sap

Joey stood in the farmyard, his head tilted back and his mouth open wide. A wild wind whipped through the evening sky, scattering snowflakes everywhere. Joey laughed as he caught the thick, wet crystals on his tongue.

Ezra, his father, said the snow was a good sign that "sugarin' time" was here. After all, they'd had just the right weather—freezing nights followed by the warm, sunny days of approaching spring. This was the magic combination that loosed the flow of sap in Ezra's sugar bush—his prized stand of maple trees.

Sure enough, they had a good sugar run the next day. Now the sticky sap dripped from spigots on the huge trees into buckets, breaking the hushed silence of the woods with a soft, steady echo.

Uncles, aunts, and neighbors poured in to help. The women and girls cooked hearty meals to send up to the sugarhouse, nestled into

Opposite: A sugar maple

a hillside above the pasture, while the run was on. Meanwhile, the men and boys hauled bucket after bucket of sweet sap and dumped it into the boiling vats.

All through the night, they tended the raging fire in the sugar-house to keep up with the sap flow. Joey stole quick naps on a cot so that he could last through the all-night vigil. Months before, he and Ezra had cut a supply of 6-foot (1.8-meter) logs and covered them to keep them dry for "sugarin' time." New logs or wet logs wouldn't do. Only dry wood kept the fires hot enough. The faster the sap boils, the better the syrup will be.

Once the best sap was gathered, the women and girls arrived at the sugarhouse with huge spoons and pans. Working in a long row, they beat the heavy syrup till it was thick, creamy, and smooth. Just at the right moment, they poured the syrup into cans and tin molds. After it stood all night, they wrapped and packed the thick syrup and succulent sugar cakes for their customers.

On a snowbank downwind from the trees, Joey scooped up a panful of sugar-coated snow where the wind had blown it far from the buckets. He packed it down flat, and he and his cousins ate their fill of the sticky, chewy stuff. When the pan was empty, they chewed on pickles to get the sweet taste out of their mouths. Then they started eating the sugary snow all over again.

After five more good sugar runs over the next three weeks, "sugarin' time" was over for the year. Soon it would be time to plow the fields and begin the spring plantings. In their spare time, Joey and Ezra cleaned the sap buckets, made repairs in the sugarhouse, and chopped more wood for next year's fires. As he savored sweet maple candy through the summer and fall, Joey remembered the excitement of "sugarin' time" and dreamed of the days when the sap would begin to flow again.

"Sugarin' time" still brings on a flurry of activity, just as it did when Joey was a child in the 1930s. Native Americans first taught the settlers how to tap maples for sap and boil it down. Today, there are about 2,000 sugar makers in Vermont. While the basic principles of sugar making are the same as they always have been, some aspects have changed with the times. One difference is that the process has become a high-tech affair. Plastic tubing now runs from the trees right into the sugarhouse, and electric pumps help speed the flow. And today, a commercial sugarbush might cover 100 acres (40 hectares) of maple trees or more.

"Sugarin' time" is now more high-tech than it used to be.

Vermont is the biggest supplier of maple sugar products in the United States, and "sugarin'" is typical of the state's rural character. Vermont is the most rural state in the country, with more than two-thirds of the people living outside the big cities and towns.

The simple, unspoiled nature of Vermont makes it a beautiful place to visit and an attractive place to live. By law, no billboards clutter the roadside view. The Green Mountains, running like a spine down the center of the state, gave Vermont the nickname Green Mountain State.

Thousands of visitors come to these mountains every year—to ski or just to watch the changing leaves. In the hushed silence of the

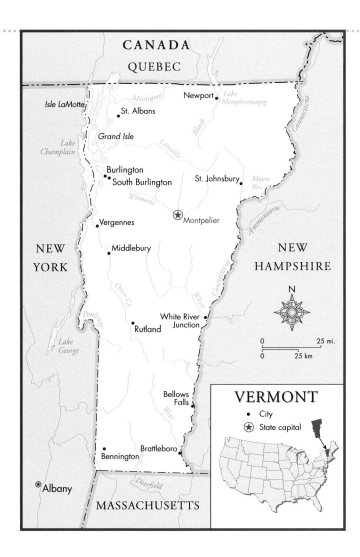

**Geopolitical map
of Vermont**

forests, you can easily imagine Ethan Allen and his Green Mountain Boys, Vermont's Revolutionary War heroes, creeping through
the underbrush.

Parts of Vermont seem to have changed little since Ethan
Allen's time. The wild forests and haunting wilderness areas seem
frozen in a time before humans arrived. But modern-day settlers,
like those of two centuries ago, are eager for a piece of Vermont's

simple beauty. Flatlanders—newcomers from out of state—buy up land for building, and housing developments and shopping centers spring up faster than many Vermonters would like.

Now the state is scrambling to balance economic development with environmental protection—to grow while preserving the land. Underlying this struggle is one point on which Vermonters and outsiders agree—Vermont's natural beauty is its greatest wealth.

Vermont's natural beauty attracts tourists as well as land developers.

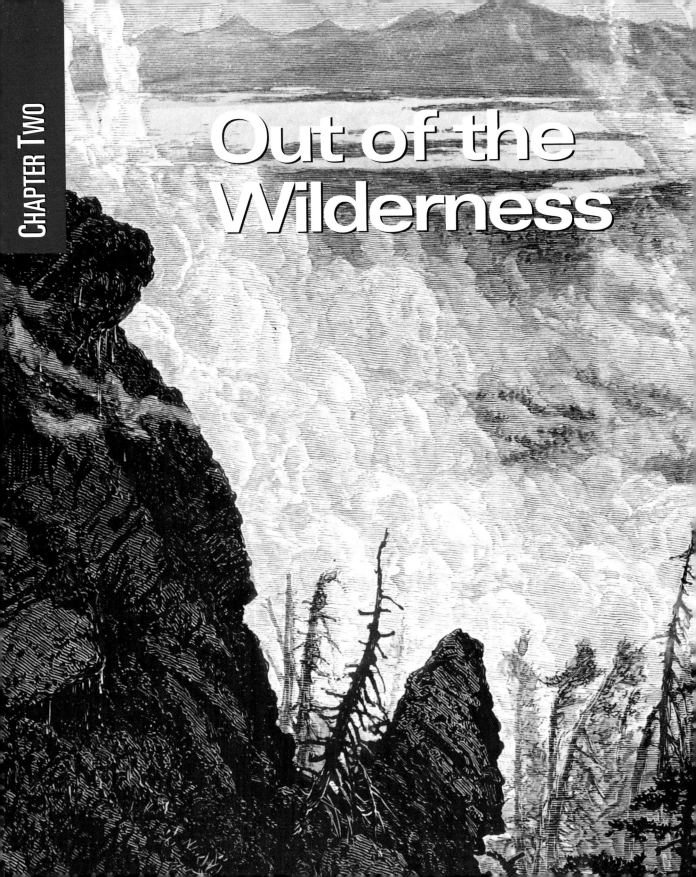

Out of the Wilderness

Vermont's first inhabitants were Abenaki, Mahican, and Pennacook people of the Algonquin language group. The Abenaki lived around the mouth of the Missisquoi River at Lake Champlain. The Mahican hunted in the west and southwest, and the Pennacook occupied Vermont's eastern edge.

Vermont was a wonderful place to live. The river valleys were fertile, the wooded hills abounded with wildlife, and the lakes and streams were full of fish. Remnants of Indian settlements have been found throughout Vermont—from villages that thrived on the Missisquoi to communities along the Connecticut River in Orange County. Some groups were seminomadic. They returned to a favorite spot year after year to raise crops, hunt and fish, and gather berries and maple sap.

Opposite: Lake Champlain as seen from Mount Mansfield

The Abenaki, or Wabanaki, lived in Vermont at least as early as 9300 B.C. Their name means "people of the dawn"—people who live in the east, where the sun rises. Abenaki dwellings were dome-shaped and covered with bark or woven grass. Their Missisquoi village had more than 250 acres (101 ha) planted in maize, or corn. Other crops were beans and squash. They varied their diet by hunting, fishing, and gathering wild plants.

Members of the Iroquois Confederacy lived across the lake in present-day New York State. In the 1500s, they began crossing into Vermont and driving out the Algonquin tribes.

A statue of French explorer Samuel de Champlain now stands on Isle La Motte.

The French Arrive

French explorer Samuel de Champlain was the first European to arrive in what is now Vermont. From Canada's St. Lawrence River, he sailed south down the Richelieu River in 1609. On July 4, he entered a huge lake and claimed all the territory he saw for France. That lake, along present-day Vermont's northwest border, became known as Lake Champlain.

Other French explorers soon followed. Gazing on the high, tree-covered mountains that run through the region, they named them *les verts monts*—French for "green mountains." The word "Vermont" came from this name.

To guard and protect their new lands, the French set up military forts. They built a fort called Sainte Anne on Isle La Motte, a large island in Lake Champlain, in 1666. Meanwhile, England had its eyes on the frontier, too. Jacobus De Warm led his English troops northward from Albany, New York, into present-day Vermont. They built a fort at Chimney Point, near Middlebury, in 1690.

In the late 1600s, the Abenaki formed the Abenaki Confederacy to defend themselves against the English and Iroquois. Pennacook tribes eventually moved north and joined them. The French helped Algonquin groups regain their territory from the Iroquois—but it wasn't out of kindness! The Iroquois were frighten-

The site of Fort Sainte Anne

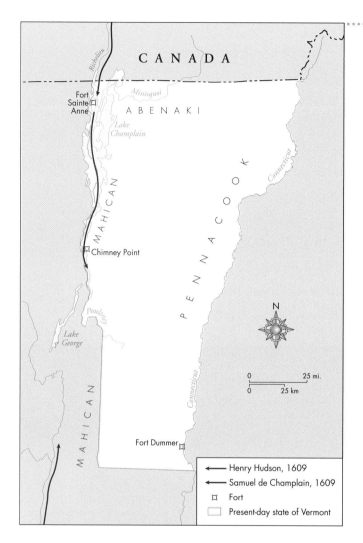

Exploration of Vermont

ing away Algonquins who traded furs to the French. Sadly, European diseases such as smallpox, diphtheria, and influenza killed many of Vermont's Indian people.

The French and Indian War (1754–1763)

Settlers from western Massachusetts moved up the Connecticut River Valley and founded Fort Dummer in 1724. The site grew to become the city of Brattleboro, now on Vermont's eastern border. This was Vermont's first permanent white settlement.

Clashes often broke out between French and British trappers and troops in this lush new frontier. It was only a matter of time until the two nations went to war. The conflict broke out in 1754, and the Lake Champlain region was a major hotbed. Though it's known as the French and Indian War, both sides used Native Americans to fight for them.

In the end, Great Britain won. In the Treaty of Paris of 1763, the land that is now Vermont became British territory, along with much of France's other North American holdings. But now the question was: to which British colony would Vermont belong?

The New Hampshire Grants

In 1609, the year Champlain explored Lake Champlain, Henry Hudson sailed up the Hudson River. His explorations led to the Dutch colony of New Amsterdam. It became the English colony of New York in 1664. North and east of Albany, New York, was a wide-open frontier. New York gave land grants to settlers who moved there.

Meanwhile, the New Hampshire colony was expanding westward. Benning Wentworth reigned as its colonial governor. Between 1749 and 1763, he gave out more than 130 land grants—mostly to his family and friends. Called the New Hampshire Grants, these townships spilled over the Connecticut River into the land claimed by New York.

The two colonies squabbled over the territory until Britain had to step in. In 1764, it declared the Connecticut River the border between New Hampshire and New York.

The Green Mountain Boys

Britain's declaration was not the end of the land dispute, however. Governor Wentworth continued to hand out land grants, and New York moved ahead with its own settlement. With or without a royal decree, people who held New Hampshire Grants were not about to leave. They even shot at lawmen and New York settlers who tried to enforce their claims.

Finally, the New York Supreme Court declared in 1770 that all New Hampshire settlers had to either leave or pay New York for their land. This was the last straw. A Bennington settler named

Benning Wentworth served as colonial governor of New Hampshire, which then included much of present-day Vermont.

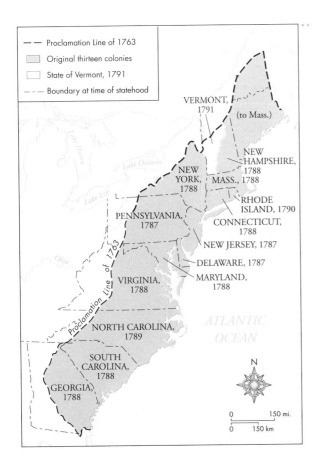

Map legend:
- – – Proclamation Line of 1763
- Original thirteen colonies
- State of Vermont, 1791
- – · – Boundary at time of statehood

Lake Huron

Lake Ontario

Lake Erie

VERMONT, 1791

(to Mass.)

NEW HAMPSHIRE, 1788

NEW YORK, 1788

MASS., 1788

RHODE ISLAND, 1790

PENNSYLVANIA, 1787

CONNECTICUT, 1788

NEW JERSEY, 1787

DELAWARE, 1787

Ohio

Proclamation Line of 1763

MARYLAND, 1788

VIRGINIA, 1788

ATLANTIC OCEAN

NORTH CAROLINA, 1789

SOUTH CAROLINA, 1788

GEORGIA, 1788

N

0   150 mi.
0   150 km

Historical map of Vermont

Ethan Allen led a grassroots fighting force called the Green Mountain Boys to drive New Yorkers out. New York declared Allen an outlaw and put a price on his head.

The Shot Heard 'Round the World

While Vermonters were still fighting over land rights, tensions between Britain and its colonies reached the boiling point. England kept imposing higher and higher taxes on the colonists. Even more than the taxes, the colonists hated to follow rules that they had no voice in making. The ever-growing cry was, "No taxation without representation!"

Both Britain and the colonies decided it was worthwhile to fight. On April 19, 1775, a colonial militia faced the British at the

Ethan Allen

Ethan Allen (1738–1789) was born in Litchfield, Connecticut. In 1769, he and his brothers Ira and Levi settled in Bennington, part of the New Hampshire Grants. Allen helped organize the Green Mountain Boys in 1770 to defend Vermonters' landholdings against New Yorkers.

In 1775, early in the Revolutionary War, Allen led the Green Mountain Boys in the capture of Fort Ticonderoga in New York. Shortly afterward, the British took Allen prisoner. When he was freed in 1778, Allen and his brothers continued the land-grant feud. Allen moved to Burlington in 1787. He died there in 1789, two years before Vermont became a state. ■

Battle of Lexington in Massachusetts. One shot rang out, and others followed. In a matter of minutes, eight colonists lay dead. The Revolutionary War (1775–1783) had begun.

That opening shot lives on in history as "the shot heard 'round the world." It's said that Solomon Brown of Vermont was the first Revolutionary soldier to shed British blood.

Vermont Joins the War

Ethan Allen and his Green Mountain Boys were primed and ready for the fight. Just a month after war broke out, they joined up with Benedict Arnold and his Massachusetts commission. On May 10–11, 1775, they captured Fort Ticonderoga and Crown Point from the British. These were crucial points on the southern tip of Lake Champlain. From there, the colonists could control the lake and move on into Canada.

Allen and his friend Seth Warner, another leader of the Green Mountain Boys, now appealed to the colonies' Continental Congress and the New York Assembly. As a result, the Green Mountain Boys were given reinforcements and made an official regiment of the Continental Army.

In September, Allen joined an attack on the British fort in

Ethan Allen and the Green Mountain Boys capturing Fort Ticonderoga

Montreal, Canada. This time, he was not so lucky. He was captured and hauled to England in chains. He remained a prisoner of war until 1778.

Independence All 'Round

On July 4, 1776, while Allen was a prisoner, the Continental Congress issued the colonists' Declaration of Independence from British rule. They called themselves the United States of America.

As for Vermont, it followed with a bold move. Delegates from towns in the New Hampshire Grants met in Westminster and made some decisions. They figured that if Britain's hold on the colonies was void, then New York's rights to Vermont were void, too. After all, those rights had been granted by Britain.

On January 15, 1777, they declared themselves an independent republic and issued their own Declaration of Independence. Now the name New Hampshire Grants was out of date, so the territory named itself New Connecticut.

British troops led by General John Burgoyne regained Fort Ticonderoga in July 1777. As the colonists retreated, Seth Warner battled Burgoyne's troops in Hubbardton. This at least gave the colonists a chance to retreat safely.

The Battle of Bennington

Burgoyne may have been the victor this time, but his fortunes fell as the summer wore on. As he marched down the Hudson River Valley, colonists tormented him by laying fallen trees in his path. Now he was running out of supplies, too.

General John Stark led the colonial fight at the Battle of Bennington.

The surrender of General John Burgoyne to the Continental Army

In August, Burgoyne sent troops to Bennington to forage for food. On August 16, 1777, they met up with New Hampshire general John Stark and his militiamen—including the Green Mountain Boys. Though most of Stark's men were untrained soldiers, they defeated the British force.

The Battle of Bennington actually took place in New York, just northwest of Bennington. It cost Burgoyne about one-tenth of his army and left his eastern flank wide open. Nevertheless, he carried on. At last he surrendered to the Continental Army at Saratoga, New York, in October 1777.

Burgoyne's defeat gave France the idea that the Americans could win, so France joined the war on the colonists' side. The fighting ended in victory for the Americans on October 19, 1781.

A Tough Little Republic

The little republic that is now Vermont had been independent since January 1777. On June 4, it took the name Vermont, and on July 8, it adopted its own constitution. Even after the war was over, the old land disputes still raged. But tough little Vermont still held its ground against New York and New Hampshire land claims.

Things got so bad that President George Washington thought of sending in troops to quash the upstart Vermonters. Luckily he didn't, and Vermont got on with the business of self-government.

Old Constitution House

Folks often met in Elijah West's tavern in Windsor to argue about politics. But on July 2, 1777, delegates from all over the New Hampshire Grants gathered there to draw up their famous constitution, making Vermont an independent republic. That's why Windsor is often called the "birthplace of Vermont." Elijah's tavern is now a museum called the Old Constitution House. ▨

Vermont's 1777 constitution was radical for its time. It was the first U.S. constitution to outlaw slavery. It was also the first to give voting rights to every adult male, regardless of race or religion, and the first to drop the requirement that voters had to be landowners.

Statehood at Last!

Ten years later, in 1787, the new United States drew up its own national Constitution. One by one, the thirteen former colonies voted to ratify, or approve it. Meanwhile, Vermont hoped to join the Union, too. New Yorkers didn't like the idea, for many New Yorkers still saw Vermont as an "outlaw."

To make peace and help its chances for statehood, Vermont paid New York a settlement of $30,000 in 1790. This certainly helped matters. In January 1791, Vermont representatives met in Bennington and ratified the U.S. Constitution.

On March 4, 1791, Congress made Vermont the fourteenth state and the first state to join the Union after the original thirteen. After fourteen years as an independent republic, Vermont joined hands with its neighbors at last!

CHAPTER THREE

Growing Up

After statehood—just as before—Vermont traded heavily with Canada. Montreal was a natural trading center for Vermont's lumber and grain, but ties with Canada involved much more than trade. Even though Canada now belonged to Britain, it had been a French colony for more than a century. Many families in northern Vermont were French-Canadians whose ancestors had settled there over the years. As time passed, an increasing number of family names, town names, and store signs were French rather than English.

Communities throughout Vermont grew after statehood became official.

In its first twenty years of statehood, Vermont's population almost tripled—from about 85,000 to almost 218,000 people. Many of the newcomers came from other New England states to start farms in Vermont. The University of Vermont opened in Burlington in 1800. Montpelier became the state capital in 1805, with a new State House in 1808.

Vermonters turned out to be good at finding new ways to solve problems. Silas Hawes of Shaftsbury invented the steel carpenter's square in 1814. Isaac Fisher of Springfield invented sandpaper in 1834. In White River Junction, Horace Wells was the first to use "laughing gas" as an anesthetic for pulling a patient's teeth.

Opposite: Belvedere, Vermont, in the late 1800s

The War of 1812 (1812–1815)

Unfortunately, the Revolutionary War had not ended America's troubles with Britain. British navy captains kept stopping U.S. ships on the high seas and seizing sailors they believed to be British deserters. Finally, the United States declared war on Britain, and the War of 1812 began.

Vermonters were in a panic, fearing a British invasion from Canada. Just as worrisome was the trade embargo, in which the United States banned all trade with Britain. For Vermonters, this meant no more trade with Canada. As unpatriotic as it was, many kept on trading in spite of the ban.

British warships did, in fact, enter Lake Champlain. They bombarded Burlington in August 1813. U.S. forces under Lieutenant Thomas MacDonough spent the next winter at Vergennes. There they built a sturdy fleet of ships from Vermont lumber. In September 1814, they beat the British in the Battle of Plattsburgh in New York, putting the lake safely under American control.

New Ways to Farm and Trade

The year 1816 was known as the "year without a summer." More than 12 inches (30 centimeters) of snow fell in June, followed by heavy frosts in August and September. Sheep —newly shorn in the spring—froze to death, and the fall harvest was pitiful. Many farm families were wiped out and took off for a new start in the Midwest.

Sheep farmers were among those who lost their farms, although many were able to rebuild their flocks. Merino sheep from Spain were introduced into Vermont in 1811. By the 1830s, merino sheep were Vermont's most important livestock animal.

Water-powered wool mills sprang up all over the state to spin the merinos' long fibers into warm woolen clothing. As the nation's western frontier opened up, sheep ranchers there soon out-produced Vermont. By the 1850s, Vermonters were switching from sheep to dairy cows.

The Champlain Canal opened in 1823, connecting Lake Champlain with the Hudson River. This at last focused Vermonters on U.S. rather than Canadian trade. Now Vermont goods could sail down the Hudson to New York Harbor. Flatboats laden with goods also headed down new canals on the Connecticut River.

At the same time, turnpikes—toll roads—were built for overland travel. The toll collector used a long pole, or pike, to block travelers from passing. After he collected the toll, he turned the pike and allowed travelers to pass.

But it was the railroads that really revolutionized transportation and trade. The state's first railroad line opened in 1849. Soon Vermont was crisscrossed with railroad tracks carrying loads of lumber and minerals to distant markets.

One of the many debates between Abraham Lincoln (standing) and Stephen Douglas (seated at left of Lincoln)

The Lincoln–Douglas Debates

Northern and Southern states at this time were passionately divided over the issue of slavery. In the midst of this turmoil, Vermont native Stephen A. Douglas, a Democrat, was serving as a U.S. senator from Illinois. In 1858, a Republican lawyer named Abraham Lincoln decided to run against Douglas for his seat. Lincoln challenged Douglas to a series of seven campaign debates, now famous as the Lincoln–Douglas Debates.

Both candidates wanted to keep the nation from splitting apart over slavery. Lincoln opened his campaign with his famous declaration, "A house divided against itself cannot stand." He believed the United States could not survive "half slave and half free." Douglas, on the other hand, felt that each state or territory should be able to decide for itself whether or not to have slavery.

Listeners' opinions about the debates were fairly evenly divided, and Douglas won the election. But the debates, published in newspapers across the country, thrust Lincoln into the national limelight. When Lincoln and Douglas faced off once again in the 1860 presidential election, voters chose Lincoln. Even in Vermont, four times more people voted for Lincoln than for Douglas. Now Lincoln would face his greatest challenge—the Civil War (1861–1865).

The Little Giant

Stephen Arnold Douglas (1813–1861) was born near Brandon, Vermont, and later moved to Illinois. He represented Illinois in the U.S. House of Representatives (1843–1847) and then in the U.S. Senate (1847–1861). Short in height, but a riveting public speaker, Douglas was known as the "Little Giant."

Douglas, a Democrat, favored making concessions to the South to keep the Union from splitting in two. In the 1858 Illinois campaign for U.S. senator, Douglas ran against Republican Abraham Lincoln. Their seven campaign debates became known as the Lincoln–Douglas Debates. Douglas won this election.

The Democrats chose Douglas as their candidate for president in 1860, again running against Lincoln. This time, Lincoln won. Douglas then embarked on a speaking tour in which he loyally supported Lincoln's efforts to save the Union. Worn out from his tour, he caught typhoid fever and died shortly after the Civil War began. ■

Vermonters against Slavery

Long before war broke out, Vermonters were active in the antislavery movement. Across the Northern states, people had different ideas about the best way to deal with slavery. The Colonization Society transported slaves back to Africa, settling them in a colony that became the nation of Liberia. The Anti-Slavery Society favored freeing the slaves into American society, and doing it immediately. Still others believed the slaves should be freed gradually.

Vermont had citizens on all sides of the issue. The state's Colonization Society formed in 1819. Branch groups sprang up in churches all over Vermont. The Vermont Anti-Slavery Society was established in 1834. By 1837, the state had eighty-nine antislavery groups, with more than 5,000 members. Nevertheless, some Vermonters were against freeing the slaves at all.

Rokeby was a safe house on the Underground Railroad and is now a museum.

The Underground Railroad

Many slaves were able to escape through Vermont to freedom in Canada via a network of safe houses called the Underground Railroad. Ordinary citizens hid escaped slaves in dark cellars and secret rooms by day and helped them travel by night.

Harboring fugitive slaves was dangerous—a federal offense punishable by fines and jail—but it was a matter of principle. A Vermont judge, presiding over the case of two escaped slaves, declared that "only a bill of sale from God Almighty" could persuade him to release the men to their Southern owners.

The Burlington area had more safe houses than anywhere else in Vermont. They included Rokeby (now a museum), south of the city, and the homes or offices of Reverend Joshua Young, John Wheeler, Mark Rice, lumber merchant Lucius Bigelow, and insurance executive Salmon R. Wires. Both bounty hunters and federal marshals constantly combed the area for escapees.

The Civil War (1861–1865)

One by one, Southern states began to secede—or withdraw—from the Union, forming the Confederate States of America. Tensions escalated until April 1861, when Confederates fired on Fort Sumter, South Carolina. The Civil War had begun.

When President Lincoln called for soldiers to defend the Union cause, Vermont was the first state to step up and offer volunteers. Vermont regiments fought in the Battles of Gettysburg in Pennsylvania, Cedar Creek and Lee's Mills in Virginia, and many others. More than 34,000 Vermonters fought in the war, and more than 5,000 were killed or mortally wounded, or died of disease or perished in prison camps.

Members of a Vermont regiment during the Civil War

The war reached its northernmost point during the St. Albans (Vermont) Raid of October 19, 1864. Under Captain Bennett Young, about twenty Confederate escapees from U.S. army prison camps rode into St. Albans. Young drew his gun, strode up the steps of a hotel, and declared, "This city is now in the possession of the Confederate States of America!" The raiders robbed three banks of a total of $200,000 and fled into Canada. Before they left, however, they shot and wounded five citizens, one of whom died. St. Albans residents followed in hot pursuit, and most of the money was recovered.

The war ended at last when General Robert E. Lee of the Confederate army surrendered to Union General Ulysses S. Grant on April 9, 1865. But the nation's relief soon changed to horror and grief. Five days later, on April 14, President Lincoln was shot and killed by an assassin.

Again, Vermonters lent their hearts and skills to a national cause. Reverend Harkness Gray of Vermont had been the Senate chaplain for many years. He was one of the four ministers who took part in Lincoln's funeral. Vermont sculptor Larkin Mead designed the sculptures on Lincoln's tomb.

Larkin Mead, a Vermont artist, created the sculptures at Lincoln's tomb.

Letters from a Soldier

Elijah S. Brown of Woodbury fought with the Second Vermont Regiment in the Civil War and died in a military hospital in 1863. The following excerpts were taken from letters he wrote to his sister (punctuation added and spelling corrected):

"The boys are beginning to have the plague here, but I haven't had it yet, but I know not how soon I shall. It is very sickly here. Some of the boys can't stand up to march more than a mile before they will fall out of the ranks."

"There was 500 men brought here from Bull Run wounded; had lain there 10 days without any care whatsoever. Their wounds were rotten. It was an awful sight to witness. They are in [the] same hospital with me—69 in the same room."

"In my Co. the [figures are] 17 killed and wounded, and Chas. Dodge is one of them, and he is probably dead, for when I left him he could not speak. The balls passed through his neck. He was bleeding to death fast. The Dr. said he would not live an hour, and then I left him for the enemy was close on to me."

"I am reduced to 128 lbs.—nothing but a shadow." ∎

Postwar Vermont

After the war, farming began to decline in Vermont. Many farmers decided to move to states with a better climate. Others were lured from farm life by the promise of factory jobs. Vermont's lumber mills, cheese-processing plants, and stone quarries employed hundreds of workers. Burlington flourished as a shipping and wood-processing center. Its port received timber from Canada and shipped out the lumber.

Still, the state was slipping backward in some ways. Its textile industry collapsed as mills moved south to get cheaper

One of Vermont's many cheese factories

Chester A. Arthur

Chester Alan Arthur (1829–1886) was the twenty-first president of the United States. He was born in Fairfield, the son of a Baptist minister from Ireland. As collector for the New York Custom House, he supervised the collection of import duties. Arthur was loyal to the Republican Party's political machine. He firmly believed in the spoils system, which rewarded loyal party workers with government jobs.

Arthur served as vice-president under James Garfield. He became president in 1881 when Garfield was assassinated after just a few months in office. It was said that Arthur "looked like a president." He was tall, dignified, and fashionably dressed.

As president, Arthur discarded his belief in the spoils system and became a champion for reform. With Arthur's pressure, Congress passed the Civil Service Act in 1883. It protected government employees from losing their jobs for political reasons and required written exams for jobs. Arthur also tried to lower tariffs, or import taxes, but without much success. He retired after leaving office in 1885 and died of a kidney disease in 1886. ■

labor. During the 1880s, Vermont's population rose by only 136 people! As one mill owner declared, "Our young men, our men of ability and enterprise, have been and are constantly leaving us."

In 1880, native Vermonter Chester A. Arthur was elected vice-president under James Garfield. When Garfield was assassinated in 1881, Arthur became president. He was the first person from Vermont to hold either of these offices.

Two Vermonters also made headlines as heroes of the Spanish-American War (1898). Commodore George Dewey of Montpelier led the U.S. Navy to victory at Manila Bay in the Philippines. Captain Charles Clark of Bradford raced his battleship *Oregon* from San Francisco, California, around the tip of South America to Cuba for the Battle of Santiago.

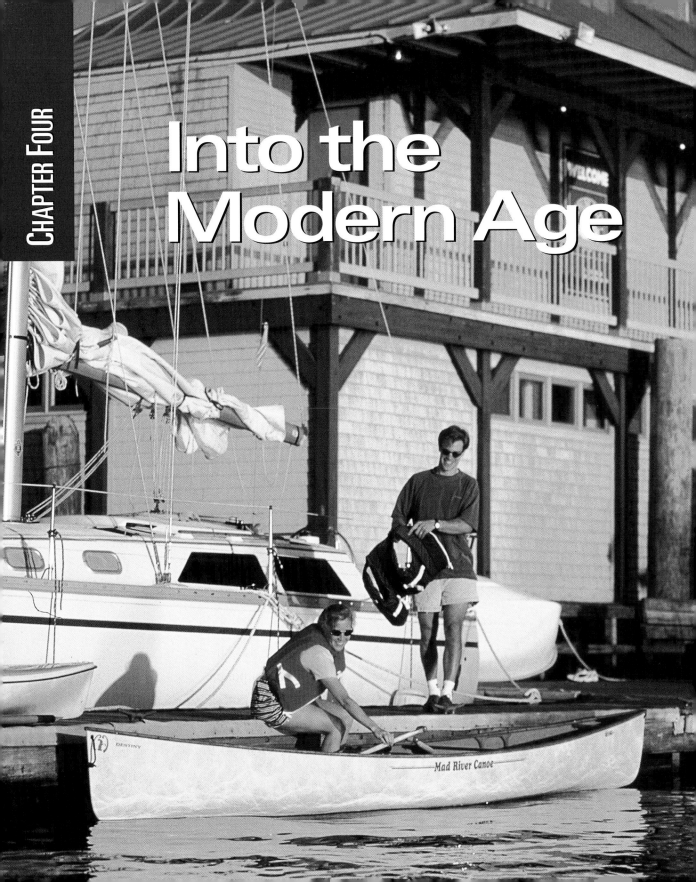

CHAPTER FOUR

Into the Modern Age

As the new century rolled around, new-fangled horseless carriages were just beginning to rattle down city streets and country roads, startling horses and people alike. One Burlington doctor, H. Nelson Jackson, was proud to own an early model. But Jackson wasn't content just to drive it around town. He set out from Burlington in 1902 and drove the contraption clear across the United States!

Now that people could drive long distances, Vermont hoped to attract visitors and make tourism a big business. Vermont became the first state to create a tourism office when it opened its Bureau of Publicity in 1911. "Vermont, Designed by the Creator for the Playground of the Continent" was the title of the bureau's first publication. This was just the beginning of the tourism explosion that was to come later in the century.

In 1920, American women finally won the right to vote. That same year, Edna Beard became the first woman elected to Vermont's house of representatives. Vice President Calvin Coolidge, a Vermont native, became president when Warren G. Harding died in office in 1923. Coolidge was elected in his own right in 1924.

Vermont's population dropped between 1910 and 1920, and barely grew at all in the next decade. Unable to compete with

Edna Beard was the first woman elected to Vermont's house of representatives.

Opposite: Heading out in a canoe

Silent Cal

Calvin Coolidge (1872–1933) was the thirtieth president of the United States. Born in Plymouth, Vermont, on the Fourth of July, 1872, Coolidge was the son of a store-keeper. His father was also involved in local politics. A conservative Republican, Calvin Coolidge served as governor of Massachusetts and vice-president under Warren G. Harding. He became president when Harding died in 1923 and was elected on his own in 1924.

Coolidge believed in a hands-off government. He left the booming economy alone, but he also failed to help distressed farmers. He served until 1929, just before the Great Depression hit the United States.

Coolidge was called "Silent Cal" because he was not very talkative. In interviews, he often answered with just a "yes" or a "no." Once at a dinner party, a lady playfully challenged him to chat. "My husband bets that I can't get you to say more than two words in a row, but I bet I can." Coolidge coolly replied, "You lose." ■

The aftermath of the 1927 flood

the farms of the Midwest, many Vermont farms were struggling or failing. Small towns were getting even smaller as young people left for city jobs or for work in other states.

Then came the flood of 1927—the worst natural disaster in the state's history. The Winooski River and other streams overflowed, washing out bridges and buildings and killing sixty people.

Depression and War

On top of Vermont's other troubles, the Great Depression struck in 1929. Across America, farms and banks failed and hundreds of thousands of people lost everything they owned. It's been said that Vermont didn't notice the Depression, it was so bad off anyway. But the Depression years saw the state's granite, marble, and machine-tool industries collapse.

To bail out the ailing economy, President Franklin D. Roosevelt instituted his New Deal measures. Vermont governor George D. Aiken made sure his state got its share of the assistance. One important program breathed new life into depressed areas by providing electricity to rural farmers. As part of the Civilian Conservation Corps, Vermonters were able to build highways, state parks, and flood-control dams.

Ida M. Fuller, the first person to receive a U.S. Social Security check

Another New Deal measure was the Social Security Act. It provided financial aid to widows and retired people. Ida M. Fuller of Ludlow was the first American to receive a Social Security check. Her payment of $22.54 was issued on January 31, 1940.

When the United States entered World War II in 1941, Vermont's factories got a new lease on life. Vermont supplied the nation's fighting forces with valuable machine tools and other equipment. Almost 50,000 Vermont men—and about 1,400 women—signed up to serve in the war. By the time the fighting ended in 1945, 1,233 Vermonters had lost their lives.

Ravaged by war, nations around the world were determined to find a way to peace and cooperation. They formed the United Nations (UN) in 1945. President Harry Truman chose Senator Warren R. Austin of Vermont as the first U.S. ambassador to the UN.

Decades of Change

International Business Machines (IBM) opened a plant in Burlington in 1956. Over the next 30 years, it grew to employ 7,500 people. Construction began on Vermont's interstate highways in 1958. Thanks to the new network of interstates, more tourists and new residents arrived.

Vermont was known as the most Republican state in the nation. But in 1962, Vermonters elected Philip Henderson Hoff as their first Democratic governor since 1854. Two years later, Vermonters supported a Democratic presidential candidate—Lyndon B. Johnson—for the first time since 1856.

More changes were soon to take place in state politics. Each of Vermont's 246 towns enjoyed one representative in the state's house of representatives. That gave towns with fewer than 100 residents as much voice as Burlington had, with almost 38,000 residents.

Such power for small towns was unheard-of elsewhere in the nation, but it didn't last. In 1965, a federal judge ordered representative districts to be redrawn according to population.

Too Much Progress?

Vermont's population and economy continued to grow in the 1960s. Ski resorts and other tourist attractions were bringing in record numbers of tourists. People from other states were discovering the joys of living in Vermont.

The state had a building boom on its hands as new housing developments sprang up in rural areas. More and more ski resorts were popping up and expanding tremendously. In 1970, faced with what some people felt was too much progress, Vermont passed Act 250 to control development and protect its environment.

In 1984, Madeleine Kunin became Vermont's first woman governor. She was one of a long line of outstanding women "firsts" in

Governor Madeleine Kunin (right) with Speaker of the House Ralph Wright

Vermont politics. It began with Edna Beard's election to the general assembly in the 1920s. In the 1950s, Consuelo Northrup Bailey was the first woman speaker of the Vermont house and lieutenant governor.

Manufacturing continues to grow in Vermont, as the state welcomes newcomers in its electronics, paper, and food industries. And tourism will probably always be a top industry in the state. Back in 1911, when the state's Bureau of Publicity opened, Vermont promoted its summer recreations. It never crossed anyone's mind that snow skiing or "leaf-peeping" might be tourist attractions! Now thousands of tourists stream in for the fall and winter seasons.

Development will be a big issue in Vermont for years to come. Factories, retail stores, and ski businesses want to expand in the state, and developers want to build more houses. Arguments rage, too, over whether to spend more state money on highways or on bike paths and commuter railroads. In the years to come, state leaders will have their hands full—balancing the need for growth with the desire to preserve the land.

Opposite: Tourists from all over the world enjoy visiting Vermont when the leaves turn color.

CHAPTER FIVE

The Abundant Land

The lush farmland of Vermont

The Green Mountain State is one of the smallest states in the Union, ranking forty-third among the fifty states. Vermont is shaped like a long, narrow rectangle that's slightly wider near the top. But at its widest point, it's only 97 miles (156 km) across.

Located in the nation's far northeast corner, Vermont is one of the six New England states. (The others are Maine, New Hampshire, Massachusetts, Connecticut, and Rhode Island.) It's sandwiched between New York, to the west, and New Hampshire, along the eastern border. Massachusetts lies just to the south. If you travel north from Vermont, you are leaving the United States! The Canadian province of Quebec lies just across Vermont's northern border.

All the New England states except Vermont face the Atlantic Ocean. However, Lake Champlain runs along much of Vermont's

Opposite: Mount Mansfield, the state's highest point

border with New York. In the past, this gave the state a great outlet for shipping.

As small as it is, Vermont includes a variety of landforms and landscapes. The Green Mountains divide the state into its eastern and western halves. Dairy farming thrives in the lush river valleys, while mountain climbers and skiers enjoy the high peaks. Geographers divide Vermont into six land regions, some of them spilling over into other states.

A scenic overlook in the Green Mountains

The Green Mountains

The forested peaks of the Green Mountains run like a granite spine down the center of the state. These mountains are the northern reaches of the great Appalachian Mountains.

The Green Mountains make Vermont one of America's most scenic—and fun-filled—states. People travel hundreds of miles to enjoy the brilliant colors of the autumn leaves. In the winter, residents and tourists alike ski the snow-covered slopes.

This long mountain range is a chain of peaks, often with one mountain rising "right on the heels" of another. The highest point in the state is Mount Mansfield, far to the north.

Heading south along the chain, you find Bolton Mountain, Camel's Hump, Mount Ellen, Mount Abraham, Bloodroot Mountain, Pico Peak, Killington Mountain, Ludlow

Mountain, Mount Tabor, Bromley Mountain, Stratton Mountain, Mount Snow, and Haystack Mountain. Killington is Vermont's second-highest peak, followed by Mount Ellen and Camel's Hump.

The Champlain Valley

The western face of the Green Mountains slopes gently down to the lowlands along Lake Champlain. Across the fertile lowlands and hills are fields waving with grain, pastures dotted with dairy cows, and orchards lined with apple trees. Here, too, many rivers and streams cascade down from the highlands on their way to Lake Champlain. Forests in this region produce much of Vermont's lumber and paper products. Burlington, the state's largest city, stands on the shores of Lake Champlain.

Vermont's topography

Green Mountain National Forest

Green Mountain National Forest is a scenic wilderness of forests, hills, mountains, rivers, and ponds. It covers more than 353,000 acres (142,965 ha), extending up from Vermont's southern border. Wildlife such as deer, bears, raccoons, and chipmunks find a safe habitat there.

Bird-watchers enjoy the many species of warblers and thrushes found in the forest. Rock collectors gather fossils, geodes, and many other rocks and minerals. Within the Green Mountain National Forest are White Rocks National Recreation Area and six designated wilderness areas. ▪

Lake Champlain

Champ, the Lake Creature

Its huge, its neck is long, and it has survived from prehistoric times—if it exists, that is. Many people swear that it does. Every year, a handful of people report sightings of the Lake Champlain monster, also known as Champ. Scientists, however, are still waiting for proof! Like Scotland's Loch Ness monster, Champ is a huge reptile that feeds on fish. Champ-watchers say the best time to spot it is at twilight, when fish come to the surface to eat insects. ■

Although New York owns Lake Champlain's western shore, most of the islands in the lake belong to Vermont. These include Grand Isle and Isle La Motte. It was on Isle La Motte that the French built their first fort in Vermont.

The Taconic Mountains

The Taconic Mountains lie mostly in New York State, Massachusetts, and Connecticut. But the northern end of the range extends into Vermont, running along the state's western edge. In fact, Lake Champlain and the Taconics form Vermont's entire western border.

Vermont also has the highest peak in the Taconics range—Mount Equinox, west of Manchester in Bennington County. Dorset Peak, Mother Myrick Mountain, and Bear Mountain also rise along this rocky ridge.

Fast-moving streams course through passes in the forested mountains, and sparkling lakes nestle in the high valleys. Stretching across the rolling hills and lowlands are meadows where dairy cattle graze. Slate, shale, and marble are among the valuable minerals found in the Taconics.

The Vermont Valley

Some of Vermont's earliest settlers traveled up the Vermont Valley from Connecticut. The valley offered a natural lowland trail between the Taconics and the Green Mountains. Bennington, Manchester, and Rutland—Vermont's second-largest city—grew up in this valley. Otter Creek passes through Rutland on its way into the Champlain Valley. The Batten Kill and other smaller rivers feed the region, too.

The New England Upland

Most of eastern Vermont is part of the New England Upland, which also sweeps up through Massachusetts and Connecticut. This region is lowest in the east along the Connecticut

Canoeing on Otter Creek

River, which separates Vermont from New Hampshire. Here the fertile river valley flourishes with dairy pastures, crop fields, and orchards.

As travelers head west, leaving the river behind, they watch the land gradually rise into rocky hills. Millstone Hill is just one of the granite-rich hills around Barre where Vermont's granite industry began. Nearby Montpelier, on the Winooski River, is the state capital.

Dairy farms are found throughout the New England Upland.

The Northeast Highlands

Granite peaks are scattered through Vermont's Northeast Highlands. Gore Mountain and Burke Mountain are the highest. Just across the Connecticut River are New Hampshire's White Mountains. These peaks, too, are made of granite, giving New Hampshire its nickname, the Granite State. This part of Vermont is sometimes called the White Mountains region— even though it's not really part of the White Mountains.

The entire northeast section of Vermont is such a wonderland of majestic scenery that Vermonters like to call it the Northeast Kingdom. Dozens of lakes and swift streams scattered through the mountains make beautiful scenery. Most of the towns here are small, and St. Johnsbury is the major entry point into the region.

Vermont Greenery

About three-fourths of the entire state of Vermont is covered with forestland. Besides being beautiful, the trees are a rich source for Vermont's wood-processing industry. They are used to make furniture, lumber, and paper.

Vermont's parks and forests

Vermont's Geographical Features

Total area; rank	9,615 sq. mi. (24,903 sq km); 43rd
Land area; rank	9,249 sq. mi. (23,955 sq km); 43rd
Water area; rank	366 sq. mi. (948 sq km); 44th
Inland water; rank	366 sq. mi. (948 sq km); 40th
Geographic center	Washington, 3 miles (5 km) east of Roxbury
Highest point	Mount Mansfield, 4,393 feet (1,340 m)
Lowest point	Lake Champlain in Franklin County, 95 feet (29 m) above sea level
Largest city	Burlington
Population; rank	564,964 (1990 census); 48th
Record high temperature	105°F (41°C) at Vernon on July 4, 1911
Record low temperature	−50°F (−46°C) at Bloomfield on December 30, 1933
Average July temperature	68°F (20°C)
Average January temperature	17°F (−8°C)
Average annual precipitation	39 inches (99 cm)

A blaze of fall colors

The best trees for autumn color are the sugar maples. The vivid color comes from carotene, a chemical in the leaves. Maples also provide the sap for making maple syrup, one of Vermont's best-known products. Sap runs through the inside of the trunk, bringing nutrients to all parts of the tree.

Ash, beech, birch, and poplar trees add their colors to the autumn spectacle. All these are hardwood species—trees that shed their leaves every year.

Pine, spruce, cedar, and balsam fir are found in Vermont's evergreen, or softwood, forests. On high windswept mountainsides, the wind and cold stunts their growth.

Springtime brings the blooms of beautiful wildflowers across the fields and meadows. During the summer, buttercups and goldenrod cast a golden shimmer across the fields. Other flowering beauties are violets, lilacs, and daisies.

Beaver Meadow Bog in the Green Mountains is carpeted with a spongy layer of sphagnum moss. This is a habitat for bog species such as pitcher plants, orchids, labrador tea, and mountain laurel. They thrive in the moist soil in the shadow of spruce, tamarack, and bog birch trees.

The Spirit of America

A majestic old sugar maple in Dorset known as the Spirit of America may be as much as 400 years old. Under its broad branches stands the home of Cephas Kent, who helped in Vermont's struggle for independence.

Wildflowers in a springtime meadow

Wild Creatures

Creatures of all kinds find food and shelter in Vermont's forests and grasslands. The white-tailed deer is Vermont's most common wild animal. Deer, moose, and black bears are the largest animals you're likely to see in the woods. The Vermont black bear might be spotted eating its favorite meal of wild fruits and berries.

These big animals live side by side with smaller mammals such as foxes, raccoons, muskrats, porcupines, woodchucks, and rabbits. The snowshoe rabbit's long feet help it to hop through the deep snow. Red squirrels live in the evergreen forests, feasting on the cones of fir and spruce trees.

Frogs and salamanders are common around ponds and streams. Beavers live there, too. They "chew" trees and branches down and place them across the water to build their nests. Sometimes the beavers' dams cause floods across roadways.

The white-tailed deer is the state's most common wild animal.

Feathered Fauna

Several species of warblers nest in the woodlands. Vireos, yellowthroats, white-throated sparrows, and ruby-throated hummingbirds flit through the foliage, too. Nuthatches shinny up the tree trunks, searching for bugs to eat.

Peregrine falcons nest on the cliffs of Mount Horrid, near

A yellow warbler

Brandon Gap, while hawks soar high overhead. Owls are another predator species.

Ponds and lakesides are alive with loons, geese, ducks, swamp sparrows, and water thrushes. Red-winged blackbirds, flickers, swallows, goldfinches, and flycatchers cruise for insects over nearby meadows, while woodpeckers and sapsuckers find their meals in the tree trunks. Species that live on the forest floor include woodcocks, ruffed grouse, and wild turkeys. Robins and thrushes often forage among the leaves with them.

Fish

Vermont's cold mountain brooks and streams are home to brook trout. Brown trout and rainbow trout live in the larger, warmer rivers. The state's lakes are habitats for yellow perch, bass, northern pike, bullhead, salmon, and lake trout.

The Morgan Horse

The ancestor of Vermont's famous Morgan horses lived in the late 1700s. He was a rugged little stallion that belonged to Justin Morgan of Randolph. Morgan was a music composer, singing teacher, and penmanship teacher. It was said that the stallion's offspring could "outdraw, outrun, and outtrot" any other horse. Within about fifty years, Morgan horses were in high demand. They can jump, trot, ride English or Western style, draw carriages, and pull heavy loads. ■

Bicknell's Thrush

The wild, cascading song of the Bicknell's thrush begins at dusk and lasts till darkness falls. These rare songbirds nest high in the thick, remote forests of Vermont. After a winter in the Caribbean islands, they arrive in New England in late May and begin nesting in June. They hide their compact nests against the trunks of fir trees, insulating them with moss. Eggs hatch by the Fourth of July, and about twelve days later, the chicks are ready to try their wings. Many fall prey to predators.

Only about 20,000 Bicknell's thrushes may be alive today. Both their winter and summer habitats are disappearing. In Vermont, conservationists fear the thrush may decline even more as new ski and mountain-biking trails come through their mountain nesting sites. ■

Atlantic salmon once thrived in the Connecticut River and its tributaries, but they gradually disappeared. Today, the U.S. Fish and Wildlife Service is reintroducing them. These fish are born in freshwater rivers and then migrate to the sea. After a few years, they return to spawn, or reproduce, in the river where they were born.

It's quite an athletic feat for a salmon to swim upriver against the current to get back home. All the dams on the Connecticut River make the trip especially grueling, if not impossible. That's why "salmon ladders" have been built at many of the dams. By springing up the rungs of the ladder, the salmon can travel up the dam to the higher water level.

Climate

Thousands of visitors pour into Vermont in the autumn. They're the "leaf-peepers" who come to admire the fall foliage. The peak "peeping" season falls in the cool autumn days between late September and mid-October. Leaves show their brilliant colors earlier in the north and later in the south.

Vermont's winters are long, cold, and snowy. The coldest weather hits the mountains and the northeast. The fluffy, white snow is perfect for skiing and other winter sports. Snowfall averages from 55 to 65 inches (140 to 165 centimeters) every year. But high in the mountains, as much as 10 feet (3 m) of snow can fall in one winter.

Springtime is cool, and summers are mild—and short. Only a few summer days see temperatures over 90°F (32°C). Even in

July, Vermont's hottest month, nights can be chilly—especially in the mountains.

Vermont almost never gets the hurricanes that devastate the Atlantic coast or the tornadoes that strike inland states. Its natural disasters usually involve heavy winter snowfalls and flooding from the spring thaws.

The people of Vermont know that winter can bring many inches of snow.

CHAPTER SIX

Hills and Valleys, Villages and Towns

The letter "A" begins the paragraph:

tour of Vermont's villages and countryside is a trip through centuries of history. Almost every spot tells a tale of early settlement, bitter conflicts, or booming trade. Travelers today can stay in bed-and-breakfast inns that have been standing since the 1700s. More than 100 of Vermont's old covered bridges still span its rivers and streams. Though most are rebuilt, many date from the 1700s, too. This historic layer is woven through a landscape rich with natural beauty.

The state is graced by dozens of quaint bed-and-breakfast inns.

The Northeast Kingdom

Vermont's northeast corner is a breathtaking wilderness dotted with picturesque farms and villages. Stretching from the Connecticut River to the Green Mountains, this area is such a jewel that Vermonters call it the Northeast Kingdom.

Native Americans reigned over this kingdom before colonial settlers arrived. On their winter hunts, they trekked through the snowy countryside in snowshoes they made from leather and wood. Today, moose sightings are still commonplace, and the haunting cry of a loon often echoes through the ancient evergreen forests.

Opposite: Small-town Vermont

The Fairbanks Museum and Planetarium in St. Johnsbury

St. Johnsbury and Newport are the northeast's major towns. Entering the region from the south, visitors usually come through St. Johnsbury. This town grew up during the railroad boom of the mid-1800s. Then the Fairbanks family founded a scale-manufacturing empire and poured much of their wealth back into the town. They donated money for such buildings as the Athenaeum library and art gallery, St. Johnsbury Academy, the courthouse, and the North Congregational Church.

Another Fairbanks legacy became Vermont's only public planetarium. The Fairbanks Museum and Planetarium is located in a splendid Victorian building, with three floors of exhibits on natural science, astronomy, and regional history. It has a great collection of mounted animals and antique toys, as well as animal mummies from Egypt, Zulu war shields from Africa, and religious artifacts from the Pacific Islands.

Newport, situated on a hilltop overlooking Lake Memphremagog, is the hub for the far-northern region. The lake extends over the border into southern Quebec, Canada. *Memphremagog* means "beautiful waters" in the Abenaki language. It's the state's largest lake after Lake Champlain—and also the alleged home of a Loch Ness–type "monster." Today, this area has a rich cultural heritage.

Its French and English communities have lived side by side for more than two centuries.

In the heart of the Northeast Kingdom is Lake Willoughby, carved out of the landscape by a shifting glacier. Two great cliffs—Mounts Pisgah and Hor—tower over the lake on either side. Dozens of other sparkling lakes and ponds are found throughout the region. Crystal, Caspian, Seymour, Salem, Echo, and Averill Lakes are among the most popular.

Other towns in the Northeast Kingdom include Lyndonville, East Burke, Barton, and Orleans. Throughout the region, visitors can enjoy touring sugar farms, hearing fiddlers' contests, and skiing. Burke Mountain and Jay Peak are favorite spots for skiers. The aerial tramway that runs to the top of Jay Peak offers a fabulous view into Canada.

Skiing on Jay Peak

Central Vermont

Granite mining opened central Vermont up to both American and foreign workers. Mining began in the Barre region shortly after the War of 1812. Skilled stonecutters from Europe filled up the town by the end of the 1800s. Now one-third of the nation's tombstones come from this area. Visitors are free to watch workers sculpting and polishing the stone.

The Burns Monument in Barre

Barre's Hope Cemetery is like an outdoor museum of fine granite carvings. Stoneworkers and their families were laid to rest there, and their burial monuments are fine works of art. Three large granite carvings stand in downtown Barre. The oldest is the Burns Monument, erected in 1899 in honor of Scottish poet Robert Burns.

In Graniteville, just outside of Barre, is the world's largest and deepest quarry for monument granite. Its sheer walls descend 475 feet (145 m) from the top to the quarry floor. The Rock of Ages Quarry Company runs almost all the quarry sites here around Millstone Hill.

Montpelier has been Vermont's capital since 1805. This area along the Winooski River was settled by Native Americans as early as 6,000 years ago. Settlers from Massachusetts arrived here in 1788. At the time of statehood, only 113 people lived in the town. Now, with a population of only about 8,500, Montpelier is the smallest state capital in the United States.

The state government does its business in the golden-domed State House. Completed in 1859, it's Vermont's third capitol. It replaced the second (1836) capitol, which burned in 1857. Inside the State House are marble floors, spiral staircases, and expertly carved wood trim.

State lawmakers used to stay in the Pavilion Hotel next to the State House. Now a rebuilt Pavilion Building includes the Vermont Historical Society. It's chock-full of photographs, documents, and maps relating to Vermont history. West of the capitol is Green Mount Cemetery. Its monuments are showpieces of local stone-cutters' talents.

The observation tower in Hubbard Park is Montpelier's highest point. It offers a spectacular view of the city and surrounding

Montpelier has the distinction of being the nation's smallest state capital.

Covered Bridges

Why are covered bridges covered? To protect the wooden timbers underfoot from rot. Vermont has 114 covered bridges of all lengths and sizes. Scott Covered Bridge in Townshend is a whopping 276 feet (84 m) long.

Some bridges were made so that railroad trains could cross a river. The Shoreham Bridge, for instance, was built in 1897 for the Rutland Railroad. Trains still cross the Lamoille River on Wolcott's Covered Bridge. It was built with a full-length cupola to vent smoke from the steam engines.

The 1843 Hammond Covered Bridge near Pittsford is known as "the bridge that went on a voyage." During the infamous 1927 flood, it came loose and floated quite a way down Otter Creek. But it wasn't damaged. People then mounted the bridge on empty oil barrels and towed it back to its original site. ▪

area. The 54-foot (16-m) tower is in Hubbard Park, a sprawling expanse of hiking and skiing trails, picnic areas, sports fields, and a sledding hill.

The Morse family has been producing maple sugar for eight generations. Their Morse Farm Sugar Works, just outside Montpelier, was once the largest maple-sugar producer in the country. Visitors can see how maple sugaring is done, from tree to finished product, and taste fresh maple syrup.

Ben & Jerry's Ice Cream factory, outside Waterbury, is another great place for a taste tour. Visitors pour in to watch ice cream being made and, of course, to sample the delicious results. Another favorite site nearby is Cold Hollow Cider Mill, where people can see apples being pressed into apple cider.

In Stowe, the 1833 Green Mountain Inn stands as a reminder of the days when this area was a popular summer resort. Now it's better known as a winter ski resort, with Mount Mansfield and Spruce Peak as the main attractions. So is Smuggler's Notch. Its craggy cliffs and narrow passes once made it a great mountain hideaway for smugglers and thieves.

Baroness Maria von Trapp, heroine of *The Sound of Music*, founded Stowe's Trapp Family Lodge. Now the grounds are alive with cross-country skiers and horseback riders—and the

The Trapp Family Lodge in Stowe

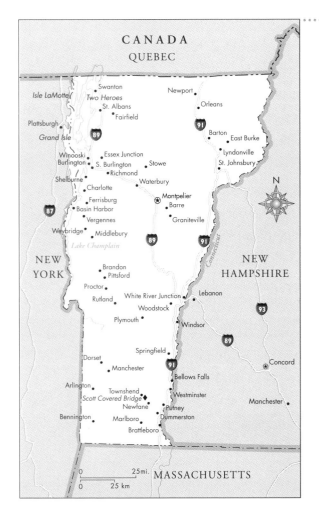

CANADA
QUEBEC

NEW YORK

NEW HAMPSHIRE

MASSACHUSETTS

Lake Champlain

0   25 mi.
0   25 km

Vermont's cities and interstates

hills are alive with the strains of summertime concerts.

Burlington

Burlington, Vermont's largest city, sits on the shore of Lake Champlain—called New England's West Coast. At the turn of the century, its waterfront bustled with activity as steamboats hustled lumber and other goods in and out of this busy port.

Now called Vermont's Queen City, Burlington is the business and cultural center of the state. Industries such as International Business Machines (IBM) employ thousands of people. With events such as the Mozart and Shakespeare festivals, the University of Vermont (UVM) offers almost nonstop cultural events.

Downtown Burlington is clean and pleasant. Horse-drawn tour carriages and outdoor artists are common sights along the street. Battery Park now lines the waterfront, and many people go there to enjoy the spectacular sunsets over Lake Champlain.

The historic Church Street Marketplace is a popular pedestrian mall lined with more than 100 specialty shops. Looming over the Pearl Street end of the mall is the classic 1816 Unitarian Church. Music clubs cluster near Main Street at the other end of the mall.

Main Street's Flynn Theater for the Performing Arts used to be an old 1930s movie palace.

Ethan Allen, Vermont's Revolutionary War hero, settled in what is now the north side of Burlington. Much of his landholdings have become the North End residential area. Allen's farmhouse, built in 1787, has been restored as the Ethan Allen Homestead. Visitors there can learn all about the exploits of Allen and his Green Mountain Boys.

Beyond Burlington

A great woolen mill used to operate in Winooski, just north of Burlington. Before that, it was the site of Ira Allen's sawmill, and now it's full of shops. The Discovery Museum and Planetarium, a science museum for children, stands in the suburb of Essex Junction. Children love crawling into the cockpit of a Boeing 747 airplane and operating the interactive computer dinosaur.

The Shelburne Museum in Shelburne, south of Burlington, is built like an early American village. Vermont's famous horses have their day in Shelburne's National Museum of the Morgan Horse. It covers their breeding and history, including some Civil War "hero" horses.

Burlington's Church Street is home to a pretty pedestrian mall.

The Old Round Church in Richmond

Huntington's Birds of Vermont Museum features carvings of more than 150 bird species. One is the prehistoric *Archaeopteryx*. Visitors can watch carving demonstrations and enjoy the nature trails and the wild-bird observation area. Photographers and architects love to visit the sixteen-sided Old Round Church in Richmond, built in 1813.

The Northwest

Vermont's northwest corner was home to Native Americans who fished and hunted along the lake and the Missisquoi River. Now Swanton is a tribal center for the Abenaki people, many of whom still live in this part of New England. Northwest Vermont is one of the state's best dairy regions, and French-Canadian culture is strong among the people in many of its small towns.

St. Albans used to be a lumber-shipping port. When trade with Canada was banned in the War of 1812, the town kept up its trade through smuggling. Later it became a railway center for shipments to Montreal. Its bank-robbing incident by renegade Confederates was the Civil War's northernmost skirmish.

As presidents go, Chester A. Arthur is not well known. But to Vermonters, he's a local hero. His restored home in Fairfield shows what life was like for Vermont's first U.S. president.

Lake Champlain and Its Islands

Samuel de Champlain was not only the first European to see this lake. He's also said to have spotted Champ, the legendary prehistoric lake creature.

The major islands in the lake are called the Four Brothers—

Alburg, Isle La Motte, the Two Heroes, and Grand Isle. Although visitors come and go, and a few orchards and dairy farms thrive, the islands retain much of their ancient wildness.

Saint Anne's Shrine on Isle La Motte was once Fort Sainte Anne, Vermont's first settlement. The site now includes the remains of the fort, as well as a chapel, shrines, and grottoes.

Elsewhere on the island are great marble deposits and what's known as the oldest coral reef on earth. It's left from the time when the Atlantic Ocean covered the area 10,000 years ago.

St. Anne's Shrine on Isle La Motte

The Royal Lipizzan Stallions of Austria make their summer home on North Hero Island. These "flying white stallions," called the ballet dancers of the horse world, perform shows all through the summer.

On Grand Isle stands Hyde Log Cabin, built by Jedediah Hyde in 1783. Hyde made the cabin out of huge cedar logs, with a massive fireplace and an overhead loft. It's believed to be the oldest log cabin in America still in its original condition.

The Lower Champlain Valley

At its southern end, Lake Champlain becomes very narrow, almost like a wide river. The hills and valleys here in the lower Champlain Valley are rich with history and culture. The towns are full of historic buildings surrounding neatly laid out village greens. The countryside is alive with deer, foxes, moose, and an occasional bob-cat or black bear.

A century ago, the Opera House in Vergennes resounded with the sounds of vaudeville music shows. Earlier still, Lieutenant Thomas Macdonough wintered here to build his fleet for the 1814 Battle of Plattsburgh. Just to the north in Ferrisburgh is the Rokeby Museum, a famous stop on the Underground Railroad.

At Basin Harbor, on the lakefront, is the Lake Champlain Maritime Museum. Here visitors can climb aboard a full-sized replica of Benedict Arnold's Revolutionary War gunboat *Philadelphia.* Chimney Point, farther down the lakeshore, is the site of the first British fort in Vermont. Programs at this state historic site explore the history of the area's Native Americans and French colonists.

Middlebury grew up around a waterfall on Otter Creek, which empties into Lake Champlain. The creek, Vermont's longest river, once powered industries in both Middlebury and Vergennes. Now the waterfall is right in the center of Middlebury, and many of the old mills are now shops. Middlebury College keeps the town vibrant with its arts and sports activities.

**The campus of
Middlebury College**

The Middlebury region's history and culture come to life in the Sheldon Museum. This old mansion of an 1820s marble merchant is full of elegant furniture, musical instruments, paintings, tools, and toys. More than 300 Vermont craftspeople exhibit their work at the Vermont State Craft Center in Frog Hollow. The University of Vermont operates the UVM Morgan Horse Farm in nearby Weybridge.

Vermonters were pioneers in developing technology to serve skiers. The Vermont Ski Museum in Brandon captures the whole story, highlighting the history of skiing and the evolution of ski equipment.

Revolutionary War soldiers once camped at Mount Independence on Lake Champlain. Today, uniformed soldiers act out scenes from their military life at this state historic site. The museum, shaped like a ship, shows how they lived and exhibits artifacts excavated from the site.

The Western Slopes

The Green Mountains cut between southeast and southwest Vermont. The two halves of the state were settled separately and grew up in their separate ways. It used to be so hard to travel between the two halves that very few people even tried.

While southeast Vermont flourished from river traffic, the southwest was home to hardy frontier families from western Connecticut. They moved up the divide—called the Valley of Vermont—between the Green and Taconic mountain ranges.

Bennington is the major city in southwest Vermont. A tall monument to the Battle of Bennington commemorates Vermont's famous Revolutionary War battle. Actually, the battle took place a few miles west of Bennington, but it was Bennington's supplies that the British were after.

Along Monument Avenue is Old Bennington, the quietly preserved old part of town. Next to Old First Church is the Old Burying Ground. Here, among the city's founders, lies poet Robert Frost. His tombstone inscription reflects his attitude toward life: "I had a lover's quarrel with the world."

Arlington was Vermont's capital during the Revolutionary War. Norman Rockwell and several other artists for the *Saturday Evening Post* lived in Arlington at one time or another. Rockwell's artwork is now on display at the Rockwell Exhibition.

Hildene, in Manchester, was the summer home of Robert Todd Lincoln, the only son of Abraham Lincoln to survive to adulthood. Robert built this twenty-four-room mansion as his summer home in 1904. His granddaughter lived at Hildene until 1975. The home has been preserved with its original furniture and the family's personal belongings—such as the 1,000-pipe Aeolian organ. Hikers and cross-country skiers are welcome to use the 412-acre (167-ha) grounds.

It was in Manchester's Marsh Tavern that Ethan Allen and the Green Mountain Boys plotted to throw New Yorkers out of the territory. A century later, Charles Orvis lured New Yorkers and other vacationers back. He made fly-fishing rods and taught people how to fish on the Batten Kill River. The Orvis company still gives fly-fishing courses and runs the American Museum of Fly Fishing.

Dorset is the home of novelist John Irving and the Dorset Play-house, known for its summertime plays. In Dorset Mountain, a few miles outside town, are some of the state's finest marble deposits. Its underground quarry covers more than 25 acres (10 ha).

Plymouth was the birthplace of President Calvin Coolidge. In his hilltop homestead, he was sworn in as president after Warren G. Harding died. Coolidge's father's general store and Calvin's burial place are also on the site.

Rutland was called Marble City in its marble-boom days. The city sits right on top of vast marble deposits. Hundreds of stone-cutters and quarrymen worked there in the mid-1800s, and railroad

Hildene, the home of Robert Todd Lincoln, is in Manchester.

The Coolidge Museum in Plymouth

Charlotte the Whale

When they found her in 1849, she was 10 feet (3 m) underground. She was 12,500 years old and far from home—150 miles (241 km) from the nearest ocean. This prehistoric whale was named Charlotte after the town nearest her resting place. Workers were building a railroad between Rutland and Burlington when they dug up her bones. Thinking they'd found the remains of an old horse, they kept on digging, smashing part of her skull in the process. ▨

cars hauled the stone to faraway markets. The marble industry declined, but Rutland is still an industrial town and Vermont's second-largest city. Several downtown buildings from the Marble City days are built of the native stone.

Nearby Proctor was named for Colonel Redfield Proctor. Stone from his Vermont Marble Company went to Washington, D.C., to build the Supreme Court and Senate buildings and the Jefferson Memorial. Today, at Proctor's Vermont Marble Exhibit, people can watch marble sculptors at work and see the many ways marble can be used.

The Southeast

Only the Connecticut River separates southeastern Vermont from New Hampshire. Settlers from Massachusetts set up Fort Dummer on the riverbank in 1724. Growing into the city of Brattleboro, it became the oldest settlement in Vermont that still exists. Now

Fort Dummer State Park, south of Brattleboro, honors the fort's original site.

Thanks to forts along the Connecticut River, new settlers felt safe from French and Indian attacks. They set up farms by the riverside and in the fertile river valley—still a prime farming region for Vermonters. With the help of river traffic, many of these communities grew into towns that still survive. Some show remains of a former life with now-closed red-brick industrial mills.

Brattleboro is now the biggest city in southeast Vermont. In the late 1800s, it was famous for two things—Estey organs and the "water cure." Estey "Cottage Organs" were a fixture in the parlors of fine homes across America. With 700 employees, the company produced half a million organs between 1852 and 1960. Several old Estey organs are on display in the Brattleboro Museum and Art Center, housed in the town's old railroad station.

Brattleboro is situated on the Connecticut River.

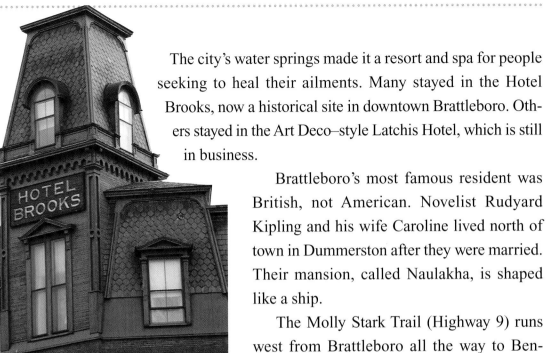

The city's water springs made it a resort and spa for people seeking to heal their ailments. Many stayed in the Hotel Brooks, now a historical site in downtown Brattleboro. Others stayed in the Art Deco–style Latchis Hotel, which is still in business.

Brattleboro's most famous resident was British, not American. Novelist Rudyard Kipling and his wife Caroline lived north of town in Dummerston after they were married. Their mansion, called Naulakha, is shaped like a ship.

The Molly Stark Trail (Highway 9) runs west from Brattleboro all the way to Bennington in the far west. Beautiful views can be seen along its twists and turns through the Green Mountains. Along the way is Marlboro, home of Marlboro College and the summer-

The Hotel Brooks in Brattleboro

Molly Stark

Molly Stark State Park is located along the Molly Stark Trail, which cuts through southern Vermont. It's a popular scenic area with mountains, woods, hiking trails, and camping grounds. Molly was the wife of General John Stark, hero of the Revolutionary War Battle of Bennington. The trail marks his route on the way to the battle. He called it the Molly Stark Trail to keep British spies from knowing his whereabouts.

Elizabeth "Molly" Page (1737–1814) married Stark in 1758, and they had eleven children. She nursed Stark's troops in her home when they were struck with a smallpox epidemic. Schools, parks, streets, and businesses in Vermont are named in her honor. ▨

time Marlboro Music Festival. Farther west is Wilmington, gateway to the Mount Snow ski resorts to the north. In the 1960s, this region was the nation's busiest ski area.

Putney, upriver from Brattleboro, was once the site of a commune based on free love. Now it's a haven for artisans and craftspeople. To the west is Newfane, famous for being "pretty as a postcard." Its shady village green and stately white church and courthouse look much as they did in the early 1800s.

The Green Mountain Boys fought a bloody battle with New Yorkers in Westminster. Two years later, Vermonters met here and declared their independence.

Settlers heading up the river couldn't get past Bellows Falls. They ran into its 52-foot (16-m) waterfall. The solution was to build a canal with nine locks. Built between 1791 and 1802, this was the first canal in the United States. Travelers used it until the railroads came along. The canal still runs through Bellows Falls, with the waters now powering a hydroelectric station. The power plant's salmon ladder enables Atlantic trout to swim—or leap—upstream to their spawning grounds.

The machine-tool industry flourished between Springfield and Windsor for more than a century. The area is nicknamed Precision Valley because of all the grinders, lathes, and other precision tool-making equipment it produces. Business has dropped off dramatically, however, since the coming of computer-aided design and manufacturing.

Springfield's Hartness House was the estate of machine-tool designer James Hartness. He eventually became governor of Vermont (1921–1923). Now his home is an inn where visitors can

The Windsor-Cornish is the nation's longest covered bridge.

descend into the 240-foot (73-m) tunnel that leads to Hartness's underground laboratory and observatory.

Windsor is known as the birthplace of Vermont. Delegates met there in 1777 and drew up their first constitution. Spanning the Connecticut River, the Windsor-Cornish Covered Bridge is the longest covered bridge in the country. Windsor's American Precision Museum houses the nation's largest collection of machine tools, as well as antique sewing machines, guns, and typewriters.

White River Junction, once a meeting point for Vermont's earliest railroad lines, is now a major crossroads for interstate highways. The road heading west leads to many fascinating sites. Quechee Gorge over the Ottauquechee River is called Vermont's

Little Grand Canyon. Hiking trails offer spectacular views from 162 feet (49 m) above the river.

At the Sugarbush Cheese and Maple Syrup Farm in Woodstock, visitors can watch the cheese- and syrup-making processes in action. Both Sugarbush and the Billings Farm and Museum show visitors a close-up view of daily farm activities. Woodstock is also home to the Vermont Raptor Center. Owls, hawks, falcons, and eagles swoop through its outdoor exhibit space. It's all part of the Vermont Institute of Natural Science, dedicated to Vermont's rich wildlife resources.

Elm Street in Woodstock

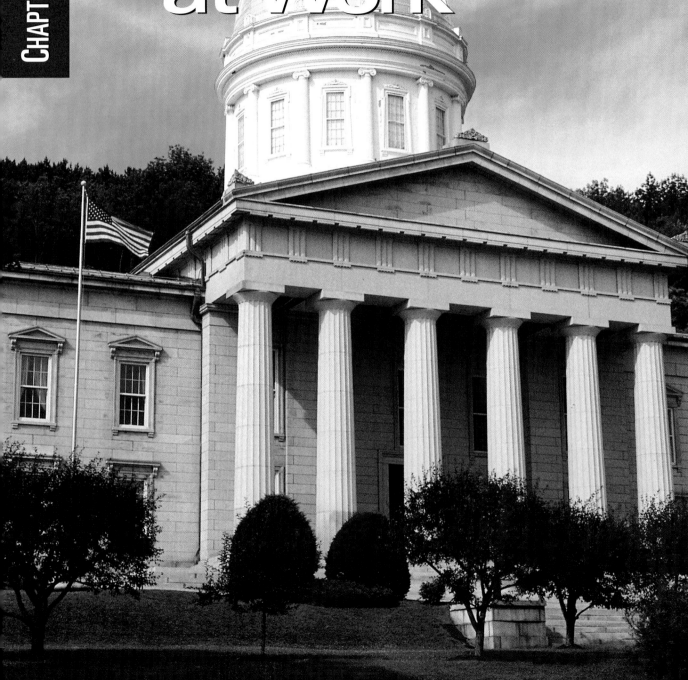

Democracy at Work

solemnly swear . . . that when-ever I am called to give my vote or suffrage, touching any matter that concerns the State of Vermont, I will do it so, as in my conscience, I shall judge will most conduce to the best good of the same, as established by the Constitution, without fear or favor of any person."

This is the Freeman's Oath, a pledge that all Vermont voters must make. Today's version evolved from colonial times, when a person swore *many* things in the Freeman's Oath—such as allegiance to the king of England.

A reception room within the state capitol

Vermont adopted its first constitution in 1777—fourteen years before it became a state. That constitution was revised in 1786. The third constitution was the one that stood the test of time. Vermont's 1793 constitution still stands today, more than two centuries after it was adopted.

How can Vermonters in modern times still live by a 200-year-old document? They add amendments, or changes, to meet modern challenges. The process takes quite a long time, though. Every four years, a new amendment may be proposed in Vermont's legislature.

Opposite: The Capitol in Montpelier

Then two-thirds of the state senate and a majority of the house of representatives must approve it. Two years later, a majority of both houses must vote their final approval. Finally, the amendment is submitted to the voters. If the majority vote "yes," the amendment passes.

Like the U.S. government, Vermont's state government has three branches—executive, legislative, and judicial. The legislature makes state laws, and the executive branch sees that these laws are carried out. The judicial branch interprets and explains the laws to make sure people understand and follow them properly.

This division of power was a cornerstone of America's idea of freedom and democracy. It rejects any notion of a king and ensures that no one person or group can ever become too powerful.

Executive Branch

Most states elect their governors to a four-year term, but in Vermont, a governor is elected every two years. That's twice as long a term as Vermont's first governors served, however. For almost 100 years (1777–1870), Vermonters elected a new governor every year! Then the term was changed to two years, with elections held in odd-numbered years. This system lasted until 1914. Since then, voters select a new governor in November of even-numbered years.

Vermont voters casting their ballots

Vermont's State Government

Executive Branch

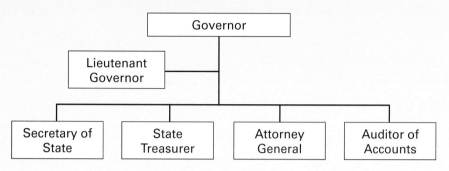

Governor

Lieutenant Governor

Secretary of State | State Treasurer | Attorney General | Auditor of Accounts

Legislative Branch

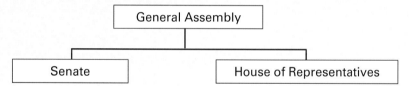

General Assembly

Senate | House of Representatives

Judicial Branch

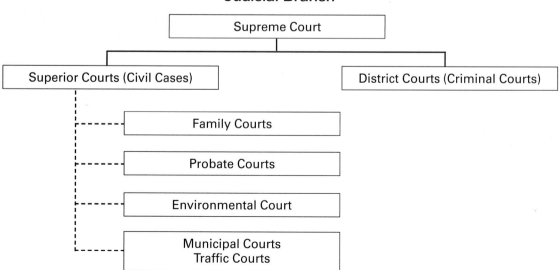

Supreme Court

Superior Courts (Civil Cases) | District Courts (Criminal Courts)

Family Courts

Probate Courts

Environmental Court

Municipal Courts
Traffic Courts

Vermont's Governors

Name	Party	Term	Name	Party	Term
Thomas Chittenden	# None	1778–1789	Charles K. Williams	Whig	1850–1852
Moses Robinson	# None	1789–1790	Erastus Fairbanks	Whig	1852–1853
Thomas Chittenden	# None	1790–1791	John S. Robinson	Dem.	1853–1854
Thomas Chittenden	None	1791–1797	Stephen Royce	Rep.	1854–1856
Paul Brigham	None	1797	Ryland Fletcher	Rep.	1856–1858
Isaac Tichenor	Fed.	1797–1807	Hiland Hall	Rep.	1858–1860
Israel Smith	Dem.-Rep.	1807–1808	Erastus Fairbanks	Rep.	1860–1861
Isaac Tichenor	Fed.	1808–1809	Frederick Holbrook	Rep.	1861–1863
Jonas Galusha	Dem.-Rep.	1809–1813	J. Gregory Smith	Rep.	1863–1865
Martin Chittenden	Fed.	1813–1815	Paul Dillingham	Rep.	1865–1867
Jonas Galusha	Dem.-Rep.	1815–1820	John B. Page	Rep.	1867–1869
Richard Skinner	Dem.-Rep.	1820–1823	Peter T. Washburn	Rep.	1869–1870
Cornelius P. Van Ness	Dem.-Rep.	1823–1826	George W. Hendee	Rep.	1870
Ezra Butler	Nat. Rep.	1826–1828	John W. Stewart	Rep.	1870–1872
Samuel C. Crafts	Nat. Rep.	1828–1831	Julius Converse	Rep.	1872–1874
William A. Palmer	Anti-Masonic	1831–1835	Asahel Peck	Rep.	1874–1876
Silas H. Jennison	Whig	1835–1841	Horace Fairbanks	Rep.	1876–1878
Charles Paine	Whig	1841–1843	Redfield Proctor	Rep.	1878–1880
John Mattocks	Whig	1843–1844	Roswell Farnham	Rep.	1880–1882
William Slade	Whig	1844–1846	John L. Barstow	Rep.	1882–1884
Horace Eaton	Whig	1846–1848	Samuel E. Pingree	Rep.	1884–1886
Carlos Coolidge	Whig	1848–1850	Ebenezer J. Ormsbee	Rep.	1886–1888

Governor Howard Dean took office in 1991.

The governor is Vermont's chief executive officer and the head of the executive branch of state government. Other executive officers are the lieutenant governor, secretary of state, attorney general, auditor of accounts, and treasurer. Like the governor, all these officers are elected to a two-year term and can be re-elected any number of times. The governor also appoints the heads of various executive departments and commissions.

The secretary of state's office keeps many of Vermont's impor-

Name	Party	Term	Name	Party	Term
William P. Dillingham	Rep.	1888–1890	George D. Aiken	Rep.	1937–1941
Carroll S. Page	Rep.	1890–1892	William H. Wills	Rep.	1941–1945
Levi K. Fuller	Rep.	1892–1894	Mortimer R. Proctor	Rep.	1945–1947
Urban A. Woodbury	Rep.	1894–1896	Ernest W. Gibson	Rep.	1947–1950
Josiah Grout	Rep.	1896–1898	Harold J. Arthur	Rep.	1950–1951
Edward C. Smith	Rep.	1898–1900	Lee E. Emerson	Rep.	1951–1955
William W. Stickney	Rep.	1900–1902	Joseph B. Johnson	Rep.	1955–1959
John G. McCullough	Rep.	1902–1904	Robert T. Stafford	Rep.	1959–1961
Charles J. Bell	Rep.	1904–1906	F. Ray Keyser Jr.	Rep.	1961–1963
Fletcher D. Proctor	Rep.	1906–1908	Philip H. Hoff	Dem.	1963–1969
George H. Prouty	Rep.	1908–1910	Deane C. Davis	Rep.	1969–1973
John A. Mead	Rep.	1910–1912	Thomas P. Salmon	Dem.	1973–1977
Allen M. Fletcher	Rep.	1912–1915	Richard A. Snelling	Rep.	1977–1985
Charles W. Gates	Rep.	1915–1917	Madeleine M. Kunin	Dem.	1985–1991
Horace F. Graham	Rep.	1917–1919	Richard A. Snelling	Rep.	1991
Percival W. Clement	Rep.	1919–1921	Howard Dean	Dem.	1991–
James Hartness	Rep.	1921–1923			
Redfield Proctor	Rep.	1923–1925			
Franklin S. Billings	Rep.	1925–1927			
John E. Weeks	Rep.	1927–1931			
Stanley C. Wilson	Rep.	1931–1935			
Charles M. Smith	Rep.	1935–1937			

Vermont was an independent republic during this time.

tant government records. These include the state archives and most of the governor's and legislature's papers. Overseeing elections, licensing many professions, and registering trade names and corporations are some other responsibilities of the secretary of state. The attorney general is Vermont's highest law-enforcement officer. The treasurer pays out and takes in the state's money, and the auditor of accounts oversees the way state agencies operate and spend their money.

The state house of
representatives

Legislative Branch

Vermont's legislature has an unusual history, too. When it first convened in 1777, the legislature was unicameral—made up of just one house. This house of representatives handled the business of making the state's laws until 1836, when a senate was added.

Vermont's legislature grew to be the third largest in the United States. While the number of senators was frozen at 30, a one-town–one-representative system reigned in the house of representatives. In 1965, every one of Vermont's 246 towns, regardless of size, had one representative. That year, federal judges ruled that the house must be cut down to 150 members. Many Vermonters mourned the change as the end of democracy.

Today the 30 senators and 150 representatives in the general assembly are elected to two-year terms. They hold their lawmaking sessions from January through April in the State House in Montpelier. While the law requires them to meet only in odd-numbered years, the legislators usually hold sessions every year.

On a typical day, the legislators may face numerous proposals and make dozens of decisions. They might hear the first reading of a new bill (a proposed law), consider new amendments to the constitution, appoint committees to study a bill, and so on.

The State Capitol

Vermont's first State House (right) was completed in 1808. Legislators sat on wooden benches in the three-story wooden building, and a cast-iron stove kept them warm. A glorious new capitol, built of granite with six tall columns and a dome, opened in 1836. But a fire in 1857 destroyed all but the outer walls and the columns. The elegant new State House still stands today. Its massive, gilded copper dome glistens in the sun, with a statue of *Ceres, the Goddess of Agriculture* on top. Ornate woodcarvings adorn the senate and chambers. In the reception room hangs *The Battle of Cedar Creek*, a huge painting honoring Vermonters' service in the Civil War. ■

Vermont's lawmakers make it easy for citizens to keep an eye on what they're doing. Each day's activities are posted on the Internet by 8 o'clock the next morning!

Judicial Branch

Vermont's court system makes up the judicial branch of state government. The state supreme court is Vermont's highest court. Its chief justice and four associate justices are elected by the legislature and serve six-year terms. Mostly, the supreme court hears appeals from lower courts. But certain special cases go directly to the supreme court without working their way through the other courts.

If someone disagrees with the outcome of a trial in a lower court, he or she can appeal to a higher court to examine the decision. But the supreme court is the court of last resort. Once it makes a ruling, there is nowhere else to appeal within the state court system.

When reviewing a case that's being appealed, the judges do not really examine what the case is about. Instead, they decide whether the lower court interpreted the law properly and followed proper

The Vermont supreme court in October 1999

procedures. If these guidelines have been violated, the verdict is void. Then the case may or may not go back for a new trial.

Legislators also elect judges to the next level of state courts—the superior courts. Each of Vermont's fourteen counties has a superior court. They handle a wide range of civil cases, such as disputes or injuries involving people's property or contracts.

Each county also has a district court. The governor appoints district court judges, who serve four-year terms. District courts are responsible for criminal cases and a few types of civil cases.

In a criminal case, the state government (the prosecutor) accuses someone (the defendant) of committing a crime that violates state law. Crimes with a penalty of two years or more are called felonies. Some examples are murder and armed robbery. Misdemeanors are crimes that call for a penalty of less than two years, such as driving while intoxicated.

The family court in each county hears cases about marriage and divorce, child support, delinquent children, and other family problems. Voters in each county elect judges to the probate court. They deal with estates—the property people leave behind when they die. On the city level, various courts handle traffic violations and city law matters.

Vermont has one other court that's a bit unusual among the nation's state court systems—the environmental court. Its one judge reviews cases involving the state's natural resources and city zoning laws that protect the environment.

The State Flag and Seal

Vermont had two other state flags before it adopted the present design in 1923. The first two—created in 1804 and 1837—had red and white stripes. Then legislators decided Vermont's flag should look distinctly different than the U.S. flag, so that people could easily tell the difference when both flags waved from the same flagpole.

Now the state flag features the state coat of arms against a field of deep blue. The coat of arms is a shield-shaped scene with a stag's head on top. Two large pine boughs curve around the sides. At the bottom on a crimson banner are the name Vermont and the state motto, Freedom and Unity.

The scene depicts a tall pine tree, a cow, and sheaves of wheat. In the distance are the Green Mountains. The stag's head symbolizes Vermont's abundant wildlife, and the pine boughs stand for the trees in the Green Mountains. The cow and the wheat sheaves represent Vermont's dairy and agriculture industries.

Vermont adopted its first state seal, designed by Ira Allen, in 1779—twelve years before statehood. Four other seals were adopted in the years to come. But in 1937, the state legislature voted to go back to the original design.

The state seal is round, with many of the same symbols that adorn the coat of arms—a pine tree, cow, and sheaves of wheat—plus rolling hills to represent the Green Mountains. Its central pine tree is an eastern white pine with fourteen branches. They represent the thirteen original states, plus Vermont, the first colony after the original thirteen to win statehood. An ancient pine that once stood on a hillside west of Arlington was the inspiration for this pine tree. ◼

State bird: Hermit thrush
(left) The hermit thrush is at home throughout Vermont's forests. It's often found on the ground or on low branches of shrubs and trees. Though the hermit thrush heads south for the winter, it's one of the first birds to return in the spring.

State flower: Red clover
Red clover grows all over Vermont—in pastures, by the roadsides, and even in the forests. It's important in the state's cattle and dairy industries because it's a favorite treat for grazing livestock.

State butterfly: Monarch butterfly
(left) Monarchs are large butterflies with beautiful orange and black wings. They are native to Vermont and breed there. Monarchs are most often seen in the late summer and early autumn. The 1987 fifth-grade class at Cornwall Elementary School first proposed the idea of making the monarch the state butterfly. That same year, the state legislature passed an act making it official.

State insect: Honeybee
Honeybees are social insects that live in highly organized colonies. European colonists first brought them to the Americas. Farmers depend on honeybees to pollinate their crops, but the bees are best known for making honey. Honeybees extract nectar from clover and convert it to honey.

State tree: Sugar maple
The sugar maple is the most popular tree in the state. In the fall, its bright red and orange leaves blaze across the hillsides. Then in the early spring, Vermonters go "sugarin'"—collecting maple sap to make delicious maple syrup.

State animal: Morgan horse
The Morgan horse is one of America's favorite breeds. It's great for horseback riding and well known for its strength and endurance. The sire of all Morgan horses was a stallion that belonged to Justin Morgan, a composer and music teacher who lived in Randolph. Today, more than 200 years later, Morgan horses show the same lovable traits as their ancestor.

State amphibian: Northern leopard frog
Also called meadow or grass frogs, northern leopard frogs are bright green with large black spots. In the summer, they hop across fields, meadows, and grassy woods, foraging for insects.

State fishes: Brook trout and walleye pike
The brook trout is the state cold-water fish—

the only trout native to Vermont's rippling streams. Brook trout are tasty and rather small. The largest one ever caught in Vermont weighed 5.75 pounds (2.6 kg). The walleye pike, Vermont's official warm-water fish, lives in many of the state's lakes. It got its name because its eyes bug out, almost like transparent marbles. Vermont's biggest walleye on record weighed 12.5 pounds (5.7 kg).

State fossil: Charlotte, the fossil whale Railroad workers discovered the fossilized bones of "Charlotte" in 1849. She was named after the nearest town. Charlotte was a white whale (*Delphinapterus leucas*) who lived about 12,500 years ago. She was a saltwater species from the time when an arm of the Atlantic Ocean filled the Champlain Basin.

State beverage: Milk Milk is Vermont's number-one farm product. It's also a symbol of all that's appealing about rural life. Dairy cows grazing on the hillsides are one of the most beautiful sights in the Vermont countryside.

State fruit and pie: Apple and apple pie Vermont selected its official state fruit and pie in 1999. The legislature declared that citizens shall make a

"good faith" effort to meet certain conditions when serving apple pie. They are: (a) with a glass of milk, (b) with a slice of cheddar cheese weighing a minimum of one-half ounce, and (c) with a large scoop of vanilla ice cream!

State rocks: Granite, marble, and slate Vermont has three native rocks that are important to the state's economy. Granite is found all along the eastern part of the state. It's used as building stone all over the world, including the state capitol. Both marble and slate are found in the southwest. Vermont's marble was used for several buildings in Washington, D.C. Slate is used for roofs and floor tiles.

State mineral: Talc Talc is formed from bits of ocean crust left behind thousands of years ago. It's a soft, green mineral found in southwestern Vermont. Vermont is the nation's second-largest producer of talc, after California.

State gem: Grossular garnet (right) Grossular garnet is really a mineral, not a gemstone. Its brown color is due to the presence of iron. The finest grossular garnet of all comes from the Belvidere Mine at Eden Mills.

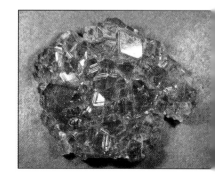

Vermont's State Song
"These Green Mountains"

Words and music by Diane B. Martin
Chosen as the state song on July 15, 1999

These green hills and silver waters
Are my home. They belong to me.
And to all of her sons and daughters
May they be strong and forever free.

Let us live to protect her beauty

And look with pride on the golden dome.
They say home is where the heart is.
These green mountains are my home.

These green mountains are my home.

Vermont's counties

Town meetings take place throughout Vermont.

The Purest Form of Democracy

Town meetings are called "the purest form of democracy." Most towns in Vermont use this form of government. Once a year, in March, the citizens assemble in a meeting hall to take care of business. They elect town officers, approve a budget, and discuss issues they're concerned about.

Vermont has 246 towns. A town includes not only the city center, but also the surrounding rural area. A few towns are too sparsely populated to have a government. Nine of Vermont's largest population centers are officially called cities. They are governed by a city manager or mayor and a city council.

Politics

No other state has been as loyal to the Republican Party as Vermont. In presidential elections, Vermonters have voted for the Republican candidate in every election since 1856, with only three exceptions.

Senator Patrick J. Leahy

Patrick J. Leahy, Vermont's Democratic senator, is one the most prominent members of the U.S. Congress. Born in Montpelier in 1940, he attended St. Michael's College in Winooski and received his law degree from Georgetown University in Washington, D.C. When elected to the Senate at age thirty-four, he was Vermont's youngest senator ever.

Senator Leahy is a senior member of the Senate's agriculture, judiciary, and appropriations committees. He is the leading U.S. official in the international campaign against land mines. Thanks to his efforts, Congress created a special fund to aid land-mine victims and named it the Leahy War Victims Fund.

Known as the "cybersenator," Leahy was one of the first members of Congress to go online and to have a web page. He crusades to pass laws that protect Internet copyrights and privacy. Leahy is also an active environmentalist and an advocate for farming issues.

In 1964, Vermont supported Democrat Lyndon B. Johnson, and in 1992 and 1996, voters went for Democrat Bill Clinton.

At home, Republicans have coasted into the State House just as easily—until the 1960s, that is. Vermonters chose Republican governors in every election from 1854 to 1963. Since then, there has been a fairly even split between Democratic and Republican governors.

As a small state, Vermont sends only one person to the U.S. House of Representatives. Vermonters showed their independent spirit once again in 1990, when they elected Bernard Sanders as their congressman. Sanders was the only Independent—neither Republican nor Democrat—in the House of Representatives.

It made big news in Vermont when voters elected Patrick J. Leahy to the U.S. Senate in 1974. He was Vermont's first Democratic senator since the early 1800s. But Leahy's 1998 race for senator made headlines nationwide. This time, it wasn't Leahy but his Republican opponent who drew all the attention. Retired dairy farmer Fred Tuttle entered the race almost as a joke. But he won the Republican primary and went on to face Leahy in the election. Although Tuttle lost, his down-home good nature made him a folk hero.

The Man without a Plan

Time magazine called it "the goofiest Senate race in the land." Fred Tuttle of Tunbridge was seventy-nine years old and a tenth-grade dropout. The retired dairy farmer became a cult hero when he starred in his neighbor's homemade movie *Man with a Plan*. Fred played a farmer, also named Fred Tuttle, who ran for the U.S. House of Representatives. As a publicity stunt, Tuttle decided to follow in the footsteps of his character. He entered the Republican primary for U.S. senator, facing Harvard-educated lawyer Jack McMullen.

Tuttle spent a total of $200 on his campaign, compared to McMullen's almost half a million dollars. When the two faced off in a debate, Tuttle clearly carried the day. To the delight of the audience, he stumped McMullen with questions such as, "How many teats does a cow have?"

But the fun changed to harsh reality when Tuttle won the primary. "Such a mess," said Tuttle the next day. "How am I going to get out of it?"

Tuttle's wife, Dottie, put her faith in the voters. "I hope they have more sense than to vote for my husband," she said. It's hard to say which of the Tuttles was more relieved when Fred lost to Patrick J. Leahy. ■

CHAPTER EIGHT

Making a Living

Placeys'
Jersey Cattle Dairy Farm

Maple syrup, ice cream, and tortilla chips—these are some "Made in Vermont" items that people all over the country know and love. Vermont is the country's best-known source for maple syrup, and Ben & Jerry's ice cream is a household favorite. Miguel's tortilla chips are found in supermarkets nationwide.

Made in Vermont

About half of Vermont's processed foods are dairy products. With milk cows grazing on hillsides across the state, that comes as no surprise. Besides milk, Vermont is known for its cheese. Mozzarella cheese is produced in the greatest quantity, but the state's cheddar is more famous. Vermont cheddar has a creamy color and a nutty flavor. It's usually aged longer than other sharp cheddars. Butter, cream, and (of course) ice cream are other delicious dairy products from Vermont.

Food products may be Vermont's best-known factory goods, but they rank only third in the amount of income they generate. Electrical and electronic equipment are the state's leading manufactures. Next in importance are printed material such as newspapers, books, and business forms. Vermont is also known for its fabricated metal products. Guns are the leader in this category, and a Burlington factory specializes in machine guns.

Showing off the finished product at the Grafton Village Cheese Company

Opposite: A dairy farm in Newbury

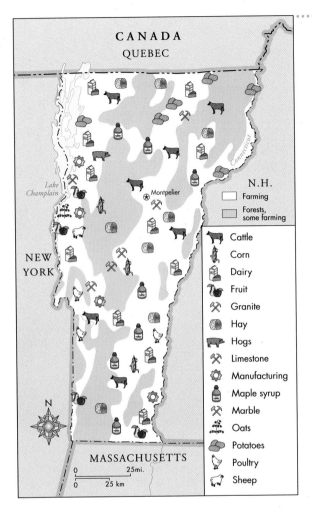

Vermont's natural resources

IBM, one of the world's computer giants, is Vermont's largest employer. Its plant in Burlington makes microelectronic chips and other computer parts. Batteries, flashlights, and ovens are some of Vermont's other electrical products.

Mining

Isaac Underhill opened the nation's first marble quarry in East Dorset in 1785. Underhill would be shocked to see his quarry now—it's a swimming pool! But he'd be proud to see what became of the industry he started. Today Vermont produces more marble than any other state.

Another Vermonter figured out how to saw off smooth, slick blocks of marble. Marble is chunky, with different-sized grains of the mineral calcite, interspersed with bands of other minerals. When marble is quarried, about half the stone is lost because it simply breaks off into small pieces.

What Vermont Grows, Manufactures, and Mines

Agriculture	Manufacturing	Mining
Butter	Fabricated metal products	Granite
Cheese	Machinery	Marble
Maple product	Electrical equipment	Slate
Milk	Printed materials	

Vermont's Finest

Ben & Jerry's Ice Cream started out in a renovated gas station in Burlington in 1978. The owners, Ben Cohen and Jerry Greenfield, had been friends since childhood. After taking a $5 correspondence course on ice-cream-making, they were ready to go! Fresh Vermont milk and cream were their major ingredients then, just as they are today.

Calling their company "Vermont's Finest Ice Cream and Frozen Yogurt," Ben & Jerry's quickly became known for their imaginative new flavors—and names. Some ice-cream names from the past include Ethan Almond, Dastardly Mash, Tennessee Mud, and Miz Jelena's Sweet Potato Pie.

Today, Ben & Jerry's factory sits on a rolling pasture just north of Waterbury. On daily tours, visitors watch the ice-cream production line in action and stop by the FlavoRoom to taste delicious samples. Ben & Jerry's is a socially conscience company. It gives 7.5 percent of its earnings to community, social, and environmental charities. ■

Marble through the Ages

People have used marble in art and architecture for thousands of years. Ancient Greek and Roman sculptors carved their statues out of white and gray marble. The magnificent Parthenon in Athens, Greece, was built of marble in the fifth century B.C. St. Peter's Basilica in Rome, Italy, is another marble masterpiece. The Italian artist Michelangelo sculpted many of his majestic religious figures out of snow-white marble. Asian artisans worked wonders with marble, too. Just one example is the glistening Taj Mahal in India. This towering monument to a beloved queen was built in the seventeenth century. ■

Isaac Markham of Middlebury hated to lose even more marble when he sawed it into blocks. But his metal saws, with their jagged teeth, only hacked off rough, chunky edges. At last he devised a way to cut marble with a "toothless saw" using water and sand.

According to Pliny the Elder, a Roman scholar of the first century A.D., the ancient Ethiopians used this same method to cut marble. Did Markham learn the technique by reading Pliny's books? We don't know. But Markham's method of sawing marble is still used today.

Much of the state's marble comes from southwestern Vermont. The marble quarry in Danby is the largest underground quarry in the world. It covers 20 acres (8 ha). Vermont marble comes in a wide range of colors, from white to black. It has been used in building the U.S. Supreme Court Building, the National Art Gallery, and the Jefferson Memorial in Washington, D.C. In New York City, Vermont marble built Radio City Music Hall and the United Nations Building.

Marble is only Vermont's second-most-important mineral. Granite is first. More granite for buildings and monuments comes from Vermont than from any other state. It's found all along the eastern part of the state and in neighboring New Hampshire. (New Hampshire's nickname is the Granite State.)

The Rock of Ages granite quarry in Barre is the world's largest quarry for monument granite. Gray granite from Barre is used for buildings and for gravestones. The granite from the Newport area is a beautiful, rosy pink. Vermont exports its granite to many other states and countries. But Vermonters don't have to travel far to see how nice it looks. It was a prominent building stone for the state capitol in Montpelier.

Some of Vermont's other important minerals are limestone, slate, and talc. Green, purple, and mottled slate is mined in the Taconic Mountains. Other Vermont slates are red or black. Because it separates into thin plates, slate is used to make roofing shingles, sidewalks, and floor tiles.

Farming—from Milk to Honey

Cows once outnumbered people in Vermont. The number of milk cows has dropped in the last 100 years, but Vermont still has more cows per person than any other state. There is about one cow to every 3.5 people in Vermont. Those cows are producing much more milk now than ever before. That's because dairy farmers keep finding better ways to feed and breed cows.

Dairy farming is Vermont's leading farm activity, and about one-fifth of the state's workforce is involved in agriculture. Milk production accounts for about three-fourths of the state's farm

A Vermont granite quarry

Vermont Visionaries

Vermont has produced an astounding number of inventors and company founders whose visions are still alive today. Here are some of their stories.

Henry Wells (1805–1878), born in Thetford, dreamed of heading west. When the Gold Rush hit California, he and his partner William Fargo founded Wells, Fargo & Company. Their express stagecoaches carried people, cargo, and bank deposits throughout the Wild West.

William H. Russell (1812–1872), born in Burlington, was a co-founder of the Pony Express. Its intrepid riders carried mail from Missouri to California in eight to ten days. Amazing as the service was, it lasted only eighteen months—from April 1860 to October 1861. The newly invented telegraph was a faster way to send messages.

Sutton native Henry Oscar Houghton (1823–1895, pictured at left) founded Riverside Press and Houghton Mifflin publishing companies. In its early days, Houghton Mifflin published works by such authors as Charles Dickens, Nathaniel Hawthorne, and Henry Wadsworth Longfellow.

John Deere (1804–1886) of Rutland worked as a blacksmith for years. In 1839, after moving to Illinois, he designed the first cast-steel plow, making it easier for farmers to turn heavy soil. By 1855, his factory was selling more than 10,000 steel plows a year. ■

income. Vermont supplies much of New England with its dairy products.

Dairy farms, like cows, are declining in number. Vermont had about 6,000 dairy farms in 1950. Today, there are about 3,000 dairy farms in all of New England, and fewer than 1,800 in Vermont. Most are in the lush, green river valleys in the northern part of the state. As in the rest of the country, the large farms are getting larger, while the small and medium-sized farms struggle to survive.

About one-fifth of Vermont's land is devoted to agriculture. Besides cows, Vermont farmers use their land for beef cattle and calves, chickens and eggs, hogs, and sheep. They grow hay, oats, and corn for animal food. Potatoes are the most important field crop, and apples are the leading fruit. Most of Vermont's apple orchards are on the islands in Lake Champlain and along the lakeshore.

More maple syrup comes from Vermont than from any other state. Honey is another bit of Vermont sweetness. Vermont's beekeepers produce several hundred thousand pounds of honey every year. In Vermont, most beekeeping goes on in the Champlain Valley. Soils there are rich in clay, which is good for growing clover. White clover is best for honeybees because its flowers are small enough for them to extract the nectar conveniently.

Vermont's maple syrup for sale

A Sheep's Tale

William Jarvis was serving as U.S. consul to the royal court of Lisbon, Portugal, in 1809. On a trip to Spain, he discovered the country's merino sheep. Jarvis was sure their thick wool coats would help them survive Vermont's bitterly cold winters.

In 1811, Jarvis imported 400 merino sheep from Spain to his farm in Weathersfield Bow. There he operated a successful sheep farm for forty-eight years. Other farmers followed suit, and by the 1830s, merino sheep had become Vermont's principal livestock animal. The merinos' long fibers were in great demand for making warm, sturdy woolen clothing. This revolutionized the wool industry in the northeastern United States. ■

Maple Oatmeal Drops

Vermont's famous maple syrup is the basis for this delicious dessert.

Ingredients:

- 1/2 cup of butter
- 1/2 cup brown sugar, firmly packed
- 1 egg
- 1/2 cup of dark maple syrup
- 1/3 cup sour cream
- 1 3/4 cups of flour
- 1 teaspoon baking soda
- 1/2 teaspoon cinnamon
- 1/2 teaspoon ginger, ground
- 1/4 teaspoons salt
- 1 1/4 cups of rolled oats

Directions:

Mix butter and sugar in a bowl until creamy. Add the egg, maple syrup, and sour cream. Beat well.

In a separate bowl, stir together the flour, baking soda, cinnamon, ginger, and salt. Add to syrup mixture. Stir in the oats.

Drop spoonfuls onto a greased cookie sheet, approximately 1 inch apart. Sprinkle with sugar and cinnamon. Bake at 375°F for 8 to 10 minutes.

Picnicking on Milk Jugs

Vermonters feel strongly about protecting the environment. As a result, they are among the nation's leaders in recycling. They're especially proud of their "plastic lumber." It's not really wood at all, but recycled plastic milk jugs. Milk-jug foot bridges, stair steps, and railings and milk-jug picnic tables are found in many of Vermont's rest areas and state parks.

At a casual glance, it's hard to tell plastic lumber from regular wood. The plastic lumber is molded into standard lumber sizes and has the look of weathered wood. It takes about 4,100 milk jugs to make one picnic table. The plastic table lasts at least 50 years—five times longer than a wooden table—and can be recycled again and again. ■

Keep Out! How Long Can It Last?

"People don't realize it's a cultivated landscape," a dairy farmer says of Vermont's wide-open spaces. "There's been a tremendous amount of work and effort put into it—the blood, sweat, and tears of farmers for over 200 years. If the farm goes out . . . it doesn't look that nice."

Vermont farmland is fertile as well as picturesque.

Acres of lush, green pastures dotted with barns and grazing cows—it's a scene that fills Vermonters with pride. It fills their pockets with money, too. Tourism is Vermont's second-biggest industry, and most visitors come for the scenery. There is even a term for visiting Vermont to see the fields of cows—"agricultural tourism."

Many farmers offer much more than scenery by welcoming visitors to their farms for tours.

Vermont is not alone in its farm attractions. Both Ireland and Switzerland are famous for their luxuriant, rolling pastures dotted with grazing animals. Both countries are well aware that tourists love to see these scenes. Their governments help preserve the farmland by giving farmers a percentage of the taxes levied on tourists.

Vermonters have been fighting for decades to save the rural look of their landscape. Banning billboards was one way to preserve the scenery. But as more and more farms close, tracts of open land are sprouting a new "crop"—housing developments and shopping centers. Studies show that the nation's farmland is giving way to development at the rate of 1 million acres (405,000 ha) a year. And New England's land is among the most threatened.

Many Vermonters are determined to keep giant retail superstores out of the state. The Wal-Mart chain first began trying to get into Vermont in 1990. At that time, Vermont was the only state in the country without a Wal-Mart store. Finally, in 1994, Vermont's first Wal-Mart opened in Bennington. But the store had to conform to Vermont's requirements. For example, Wal-Marts are usually built on vacant land far outside towns, but this store was located in a city shopping center.

Wal-Mart would like to build more stores in Vermont, and citizens' opinions remain widely split on the question. Preservationists feel that retail giants tear up the landscape, ruin the environment, and look ugly in Vermont's picturesque, small-town setting. Another important issue for Vermonters is preserving the downtown shopping areas of villages and small towns. When out-lying superstores attract shoppers away from the downtown area, local businesses are forced to close.

Other Vermonters feel that they deserve to shop at the super-stores for a bigger choice of items and lower prices. In a 1993 poll, 45 percent of the respondents wanted to keep large retailers out, while 44 percent wanted them in.

Getting Around in Vermont

Getting stuck in the snow is a typical feature of Vermont life in the winter. Rather than being a disaster, it brings out the best in Ver-monters, proving how naturally neighborly they are. Total strangers become friends in need—pushing, pulling, or dragging a vehicle with chains to get it rolling again.

Helping move a car stuck in snow

Vermont has about 14,000 miles (22,530 km) of roadways. Interstate highways came through in the 1960s. Now Interstate 89 crosses from New Hampshire into Vermont at White River Junction. Then it runs in a ragged diagonal line up to the far northwest corner, where it crosses the Canadian border. Interstate 91 enters Vermont from Massachusetts on the south. It hugs the Connecticut River along the eastern border, continuing on up into Canada. On the way, it's joined by New Hampshire's Interstate 93 near St. Johnsbury.

New Yorkers can make an easy getaway to south-central Vermont's ski areas. The Ethan Allen Express, a daily Amtrak passenger train, connects Albany and New York City to Rutland. Another train makes daily runs all the way through the state to New York City. From St. Albans in the far north, it passes through Essex Junction, Montpelier, and Bellows Falls to Springfield, Massachusetts, and on to New York.

Burlington International Airport is the state's largest. Nonstop flights run between this hub and several U.S. cities. Four major international airlines provide regular service between Burlington and foreign countries. Smaller airfields serve dozens of other Vermont towns.

Spreading the Word

The *Vermont Gazette*, the state's first newspaper, was published in Westminster from 1791 to 1793. The famous old printing press on which it was printed was the first printing press in the United States.

The *Rutland Herald* is Vermont's oldest newspaper still in existence. James Lyon began publishing it in 1794 as *The Farmer's Library of Vermont's Political and Historical Register.* For Lyon, newspapers ran in the family. His father, Matthew, had published a short-lived political newspaper called *The Scourge of Aristocracy and Repository of Important Political Truth.* Thanks to his unflattering editorials about President John Adams, Matthew ended up in jail. In 1794, the younger Lyon sold his newspaper to Reverend Samuel Williams, who changed its name to the *Rutland Herald.*

Today about forty newspapers are published in Vermont, and about ten of them are daily papers. The largest dailies are the *Rutland Herald* and the *Burlington Free Press*, established in 1827. Some of Vermont's other newspapers are the *Addison Independent,* the *Caledonian Record,* the *St. Albans Messenger*, and the *Vermont Times.*

Vermont entered the broadcasting world in 1930, when Rutland's WSYB radio station went on the air. WCAX-TV, now Channel 3, began broadcasting in 1954 as Vermont's first television station. Now Vermont's seven TV stations also include WPTZ (Channel 5) and Vermont Public Television. Vermonters have a well-rounded viewing choice because they receive many stations broadcast from nearby states.

CHAPTER NINE

People Who Built Vermont

Vermont's atmosphere is attractive to people of all backgrounds.

Vermonters will do nothing you *tell* them to do, but they'll do almost anything you *ask* them to do."

That's an old expression that handily sums up Vermonters' traditional character. Even before they set up an independent republic, Vermonters were known for thinking and acting independently. They also have a long-standing reputation for being hardy, hardworking, and thrifty—both with money and with words! President Calvin ("Silent Cal") Coolidge, a man of few words, is the most famous example of Vermonters' quiet ways.

At the same time, these people have a deep sense of neighborly goodwill. Because they know what it's like to struggle for survival on the land, Vermonters are always ready to help out someone in need.

Opposite: A young Vermonter

Population of Vermont's Major Cities (1990)

City	Population
Burlington	39,127
Rutland	18,230
South Burlington	12,809
Bennington	9,532
Barre	9,482
Brattleboro	8,612

Where Did Vermonters Come From?

Plenty of Vermonters today can boast that their families have lived there for eight generations, or even more. Many are descendants of Vermont's early settlers—those who came from Connecticut, Massachusetts, New Hampshire, and New York in the 1700s. These people of English, Scotch-Irish, or Dutch descent had lived in the original colonies until the land began to get overcrowded. Moving into Vermont gave them a chance to make a new start in a brand-new, wide-open territory.

People from Canada had been crossing into northern Vermont since the 1700s, but almost all of them left after the French and Indian War. A new wave of Canadian immigrants began arriving in the early 1800s. Most were French-speaking people from the Canadian province of Quebec. These farmers, loggers, and merchants permeated the north with French language and culture. French-Canadians also settled in larger towns such as Burlington and Winooski.

As industries began to develop in the new state, several waves of European immigrants poured in to take jobs. Eventually, they earned enough to bring their families across the Atlantic Ocean and make a new life for themselves in Vermont. In the early 1800s, Irish workers arrived to help build Vermont's first railroads. By 1850, Irish people made up about 50 percent of Vermont's foreign-born population and 5 percent of the total population.

As the granite and marble industries began to flourish, there was a great need for expert stonecutters. Artisans from Italy and Scotland arrived to work in the Barre area's quarries and stone-cutting facilities. Many of the Scots came from Aberdeen, Scotland—a large granite-quarrying region—while Italians hailed from northern Italy's quarries. The slate industry in far-western Vermont attracted newcomers from Wales.

New manufacturing industries brought in more immigrants to work in Vermont's machine shops and mills. A wave of Slavic people settled in the factory towns of Windsor County. People from Poland, Russia, and Czechoslovakia were among the first immigrants to work in the quarry towns of Rutland County. Swedish and Austrian workers joined them later.

The 1990 census counted about 3,600 Hispanic people and fewer than 2,000 African-Americans in Vermont. Vermont's Native Americans numbered only about 1,700 in the same census year. The state is also home to people who came from China, Korea, India, Japan, and other parts of Asia and the Pacific Islands.

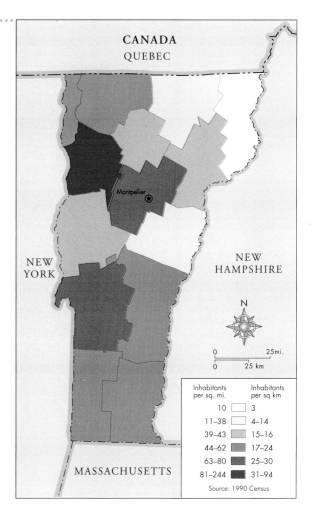

Vermont's population density

Immigration patterns of the past created the face of present-day Vermont. More than one-fourth of Vermonters today claim French or French-Canadian ancestry. English ancestry is not far behind, with about one-fifth of the population. Descendants of Irish, Italian, Scottish, and Polish immigrants are next.

Of course, almost all Vermonters speak English in their everyday school and business lives. But for many, it's quite another story when they're at home among family and close friends. That's

Burlington is the state's largest city.

where Vermont's ethnic diversity really shows. More than 17,000 Vermonters reported that French is the language they speak at home. About 3,200 speak Spanish at home, and about 2,700 speak German. Italian and Polish are the next most common home languages.

Vermont's Native Americans

Vermont's western Abenaki group once numbered about 10,000 people. Now about 2,500 western Abenaki remain in Vermont and New Hampshire. Most belong to the Sokoki/St. Francis Band of the Abenaki Nation in northwestern Vermont. However, the federal government does not recognize them as an official tribe with an assigned reservation. They are among the nation's 245 federally nonrecognized tribes, most of which are petitioning for federal status.

The Pennacook were important members of the Abenaki Confederation in the 1700s. Many of their descendants live among the

Abenaki today. The Mahicans, whose homeland once included Vermont, are now concentrated in reservations in Wisconsin.

The Sokoki/St. Francis Band set up a tribal council in 1976 in Swanton, a town in the northwest near Lake Champlain. The state of Vermont at first recognized the band but later withdrew its recognition. In 1982 the Sokoki/St. Francis Band applied for federal recognition, and they are still waiting.

Religion

In 1776, almost two-thirds of Vermont church members belonged to the Congregationalist Church. This Protestant religious group dominated many of the original colonies at that time. Now only about 4 percent of Vermonters are Congregationalists. Their church is known today as the United Church of Christ (UCC). But they have more houses of worship in Vermont than any other religion.

As more and more immigrants arrived, they brought their religions with them. Roman Catholics from Ireland, Italy, and other Catholic countries—including Canada's province of Quebec—gradually outnumbered Vermont's traditional Protestants.

Roman Catholics now make up the largest religious body in Vermont. More than 35 percent of Vermonters claim

A Catholic church made of Vermont marble

Joseph Smith

Joseph Smith (1805–1844) was born in Sharon, Vermont. He claimed that he was called to be a prophet and was given a sacred religious record that had never been revealed before. This Book of Mormon told of Jesus Christ's appearance in North America in the fifth century to establish his church. Smith claimed to have authority from the apostles to re-establish that church. Hence he founded the Church of Jesus Christ of Latter-day Saints.

Smith gained converts quickly. He soon made the decision to move West, and in 1840 founded the Mormon city of Nauvoo, Illinois. He was imprisoned for conspiracy in Carthage, Illinois, and was killed by an angry mob that broke into the jail.

A 38-foot (11.6-m) granite monument stands at Smith's birthplace memorial in Sharon. It is one of the largest solid-shaft granite monuments in the world. ■

the Catholic faith. Other religions are far behind. The second-largest is the United Methodist Church, with about 5 percent of the population, followed by Congregationalists. The Episcopal and Baptist Churches are the next largest. About 1 percent of Vermonters follow the Jewish faith.

All other religions claim less than 1 percent of Vermont's population, including Mormons, or members of the Church of Jesus Christ of Latter-day Saints. The Mormon church's two great leaders—Joseph Smith and Brigham Young—were both born in Vermont. However, they built up their followings in the Midwest and West.

Vermonters hold dozens of other religious beliefs. But there's one religious viewpoint that reflects the state's traditional independence more than any other. Almost 13 percent of Vermonters claim that they belong to no religion at all.

The American Moses

Brigham Young (1801–1877) was the second president of the Church of Jesus Christ of Latter-day Saints. Born in Whitingham, Vermont, he converted from Methodism to Mormonism in 1832. Young is sometimes called the "American Moses." He organized 16,000 Mormons from Missouri and Illinois and led them in an "Exodus" to the "Promised Land" of Utah Territory. There he founded Salt Lake City, still the headquarters of the Mormon Church. Young served as church president from 1844 until his death. Brigham Young University in Salt Lake City was established under his direction. ■

Population Patterns

About 591,000 people live in Vermont, according to the U.S. Census Bureau's 1998 estimates. Although the state lost a lot of residents in the Depression years, the population has been growing in the last few decades. It increased by 14 percent in the 1960s, 15 percent in the 1970s, and more than 10 percent in the 1980s.

In spite of its growth, Vermont's population ranks next to last among the fifty states. Only Wyoming has fewer residents. By the year 2025, it's estimated that Vermont's population will number around 678,000 people. While that seems high by Vermont standards—it's almost double the 1900 population—it would be the lowest state population in the nation.

Vermont is the "most rural" of all the states. More than 70 percent of Vermonters live in rural areas—that is, outside of cities and towns of 2,500 people. That's a major difference in living patterns, compared to the rest of the United States. All the states—except Vermont and Maine—have more people living in urban areas than in rural areas.

Vermont is comprised of a collection of many small towns.

Cities, Towns, and Villages

Officially, Vermont has 9 cities, 246 towns, 49 villages, and many unincorporated areas. An unincorporated area might be larger than most cities.

Burlington is Vermont's largest city. Located on the banks of Lake Champlain, it's a busy shipping and distribution center. More than 25 percent of all Vermonters live in Burlington's metropolitan area.

The city of Burlington itself had a population of 39,127 in 1990. That's more than twice as many people as in Rutland, the second-largest city. Rutland thrives on the marble industry and the manufacture of scales and electrical equipment.

Next in size is Bennington, Vermont's largest unincorporated community. The village of South Burlington, the town of Brattleboro, the city of Barre, the village of Essex Junction, and the cities of Montpelier and St. Albans are the next largest.

Bennington and Brattleboro are southern Vermont's biggest communities. Barre is the center of the state's granite industry. Nearby Montpelier, with a 1990 population of 8,247, is the smallest state capital in the United States. Essex Junction, just outside of Burlington, is the largest village in the state.

Education

State law requires school attendance from age seven through fifteen. About 105,000 students are enrolled in Vermont's 350 public schools, from kindergarten through twelfth grade.

Act 60

No Vermont law has caused more of an uproar than Act 60. Passed in 1997, Act 60 is a school-funding law—the Vermont Equal Educational Opportunity Act. It aims to give an equal amount of money to all the public schools in the state, regardless of whether they are in wealthy or poor communities.

In the past, each local school district paid for its schools with property taxes on local residents. Well-to-do communities with expensive homes had much more money for their schools than lower-income districts. Under the new plan, Vermont set property taxes at the same rate statewide. Those taxes are then equally divided among the state's schools.

As a result, about 80 percent of Vermont's towns are now "receiving towns"—they get more money back than the townspeople pay. Wealthier towns, on the other hand, are paying higher taxes and getting less back. In some upper-class communities, school funding has been cut by 50 percent or more.

Unfortunately, the issue is ripping the state apart. While receiving towns are making long-overdue school repairs and improvements, contributing towns have filed numerous lawsuits against the state. They feel that Act 60 unfairly robs their children of a good education. ■

Vermont's first college was the University of Vermont (UVM) in Burlington. Ira Allen convinced the state legislature to build it in 1791, the year of statehood. But the school was not ready to admit students until 1800. The first graduating class—the class of 1804—consisted of four students!

About 9,000 students attend UVM's undergraduate and graduate schools today. A few of them might say that the abbreviation UVM stands for University of Vert Mont, the old French term for Green Mountain. But it really stands for *Universitas Viridis Montis*—Latin for "University of the Green Mountain." Among the state's private colleges, the best known are Middlebury College and Bennington College.

The University of Vermont is in Burlington.

CHAPTER TEN

Food for the Soul

"*The woods are lovely, dark and deep.*
But I have promises to keep,
And miles to go before I sleep,
And miles to go before I sleep."
—From "Stopping by Woods on a Snowy Evening,"
by Robert Frost

Poet Robert Frost shared with the world his joy in the beauty of New England's country-side. He made his summer home in a log cabin in Ripton. There he helped establish Middlebury College's Bread Loaf Writers' Conference, a school for aspiring writers, and also made regular appearances. The college still holds the conference every year on its Bread Loaf Mountain campus in Ripton. It has helped nourish the careers of some of the country's greatest writers.

Vermonters liked Frost's dry humor and good sense, and so did the rest of the country. By the 1920s, he was one of the most popular poets in America. He was awarded four Pulitzer Prizes for poetry. Frost was invited to compose and read a poem at the inauguration of President John F. Kennedy in 1961.

Author Dorothy Canfield Fisher (1879–1958) was born in Kansas, but eventually she chose to live in Arlington. Her family had been among the town's earliest settlers. Fisher glorified rural Vermont life in her novels and short stories. *Vermont Tradition: The Biography of an Outlook on Life* is one of her best-loved works.

Robert Frost had a summer house in Ripton.

Opposite: Snowboard-ing at Sugarbush

Fisher was much more than just a writer. She helped make the Montessori teaching method popular in the United States. In the 1920s, she became one of the founders of the Book-of-the-Month Club.

Other Transplants and Exiles

Vermont seems to be a magnet for great writers. Over the years, many other authors who built their careers in other places ended up adopting Vermont as a home.

The British author Rudyard Kipling (1865–1936) lived in a mansion near Brattleboro for four years. Novelist Sinclair Lewis (1885–1951) lived in the eastern town of Barnard in the 1930s. He was America's first winner of the Nobel Prize for literature, Lewis's best-known works include *Main Street, Babbitt,* and *Elmer Gantry*—all of them attacking hypocrites and cowards. His novel *It Can't Happen Here* is set in Vermont.

Robert Penn Warren (1905–1989) also had a home in Vermont. Although he was a Pulitzer Prize–winning poet, he was better known as a novelist. His novel *All the King's Men* won a Pulitzer Prize for fiction in 1947. Wallace Stegner (1909–1993) kept a summer home in Greensboro. Parts of his novel *Crossing to Safety* are set in Vermont.

In the former Soviet Union, Aleksandr Solzhenitsyn (born in 1918) bitterly criticized his government. His first novel was *One Day in the Life of Ivan Denisovich*, for which he won the 1970 Nobel Prize for literature. Four years later, he was deported to Germany, where he completed *The Gulag Archipelago.*

In 1976, Solzhenitsyn settled on a secluded hillside estate near

Rudyard Kipling

Cavendish, Vermont. This snowy, wooded region reminded him of the homeland he left behind. There he wrote *The Red Wheel,* a history of the 1917 Russian revolution. He returned to Russia in 1994 after the collapse of the Soviet Union.

Novelist John Irving, born in New Hampshire in 1942, now makes his home in Vermont. He became an instant success with *The World According to Garp* (1978). This popular, offbeat novel became a blockbuster movie. His novel *The Cider House Rules* (1985) hit the silver screen in 1999. Howard Mosher, Grace Paley, and Jamaica Kincaid are among the other well-known writers living in Vermont.

Author John Irving at home in Vermont

"The Hills Are Alive"

"The hills are alive with the sound of music." This memorable tune from the hit movie *The Sound of Music* has a special meaning for Vermonters. The movie tells the gripping tale of the musical von Trapp family, who escaped the Nazis in 1938.

A year later, on a singing tour of the United States, the von Trapps discovered Stowe. The mountain village reminded them of the home they left behind in their native Austria, and they made a new home there. A few years later, and the hills of Vermont were alive with the sound of music. Maria von Trapp opened a music camp. Now Johannes, the youngest child of the family, runs a lodge on the estate, where music fills the air every evening.

In 1934, a group of musicians met in Woodstock to discuss a fantastic dream—a statewide symphony orchestra. Instead of settling in one big city, they were dedicated to bringing music to the folks of rural Vermont. They performed at gyms, racetracks, hill-

Moonlight in Vermont

"Moonlight in Vermont" was a popular song of the 1940s and 1950s. Written by Johnny Blackburn and Karl Suessdorf, it was a favorite of Frank Sinatra, Ella Fitzgerald, and dozens of other popular singers. Margaret Whiting first recorded the song in 1944, and it comforted millions of servicemen fighting in World War II.

There are people who have visited Vermont *just because of* this song's haunting melody and enchanting lyrics. The lyrics are unusual for a song of that period—there are no rhyming lines! Many Vermonters would like "Moonlight in Vermont" to be the state song. However, musical experts and the state legislature do not consider it suitable because it doesn't have a "marching" rhythm. ■

sides—anywhere an audience might gather. The musicians were barbers, mail carriers, farmers, and anyone else who shared the vision. That's how the Vermont Symphony Orchestra was born.

Art and Artists

There are still folks in Arlington who posed for the beloved artist Norman Rockwell. His scenes from everyday life appeared regularly on the covers of *The Saturday Evening Post.* Even today, you're likely to see copies of Rockwell's paintings in doctors' offices!

Rockwell lived for many years in Arlington, often using his friends and neighbors as models. His magazine-cover art and other prints are on display in Arlington's Norman Rockwell Exhibition.

One of Vermont's native-born artists was William Morris Hunt (1824–1879) of Brattleboro. He opened an art school in Boston, Massachusetts, and painted huge murals in the New York State capitol.

Sculptor Hiram Powers (1805–1873), born near Woodstock,

Norman Rockwell at work

The Shelburne Museum

Built like an early American village, the Shelburne Museum spreads across more than 45 acres (18 ha). It's one of the country's largest collections of early American artifacts, with more than 80,000 items on display on its grounds and in its thirty-seven buildings.

Visitors get an idea of how pioneers lived when they see the early carriages, duck decoys, weathervanes, tools, and quilts. There are antique toys, furniture, rugs, and china, too. The side-wheel steamboat *Ticonderoga*, a covered bridge, and a steam engine are just a few of its other art and history exhibits. ■

moved to Italy at age thirty-two and lived there the rest of his life. His sculpture *Greek Slave* became one of the most popular statues in the world and was widely copied. Powers's statues of Benjamin Franklin, Thomas Jefferson, and other statesmen stand in the Capitol in Washington, D.C.

Sculptor Larkin Mead (1835–1910) grew up in Chesterfield. His massive statue of Ethan Allen looms in Vermont's state capitol. A duplicate Allen statue stands in Statuary Hall in Washington, D.C. As his greatest work, Mead sculpted Abraham Lincoln's memorial monument in Springfield, Illinois.

Sports Year-Round

Any season of the year is a good time to enjoy Green Mountain National Forest. The first fishing days of spring bring anglers out to the ponds and brooks after a long winter wait. Summer is a great time for camping in the forest, hiking the 500 miles (805 km) of footpaths, and canoeing the rivers. Winter brings out the skiers, snowmobilers, and snowboarders.

Burlington has a minor-league baseball team, but Vermont has no big-league professional sports teams. However, winter sports are

Fishing in White River

Bill Koch

Bill Koch of Guilford, born in 1955, was the first American man to become highly accomplished in cross-country skiing. In 1976, he became the first American Olympic medalist in the sport, taking home a silver medal in the 30-kilometer cross-country race. In 1982, Koch was the first American male to win the Nordic World Cup. ■

a way of life for many residents. In the early 1900s, children in Vermont used to make their way to their one-room schoolhouses on skis. Now cross-country skiing is one of Vermont's most popular cold-weather sports. The first American to win an Olympic medal in Nordic skiing was Bill Koch of Guilford, in 1976.

From top to bottom, Vermont is full of ski areas. Some of them rank among the most famous in the world. Killington, called the "Beast of the East," is the region's largest ski resort. Close by are Pico, Bear Mountain, Sky Peak, and many others.

The ski resort of Stratton is known for more than skiing. It's the birthplace of snowboarding. Stratton hosts the U.S. Open snowboarding competition every March.

Native Americans invented snowshoes so they could hunt in the deep snow. Now, even in winter, dedicated hikers can travel the trails in snowshoes. The Long Trail is a great challenge for serious

hikers. It's part of the Appalachian Trail that stretches from Maine to Georgia. The Long Trail runs through Vermont from north to south for about 265 miles (426 km).

Cross-country skiing is one way Vermonters enjoy the great out-doors.

You could almost say that Vermont is all things to all people. The beautiful mountains and rolling countryside that make it so attractive to artists and writers make a magnificent playground, too. No other state offers such a perfect arena for both fine arts and popular sports—a place that's exhilarating for the body and nurturing to the soul.

Timeline

United States History

The first permanent English settlement is established in North America at Jamestown. **1607**

Pilgrims found Plymouth Colony, the second permanent English settlement. **1620**

America declares its independence from Britain. **1776**

The Treaty of Paris officially ends the Revolutionary War in America. **1783**

The U.S. Constitution is written. **1787**

The Louisiana Purchase almost doubles the size of the United States. **1803**

The United States and Britain fight the War of 1812. **1812–15**

Vermont State History

1609 French explorer Samuel de Champlain sails down the Richelieu River and claims Vermont for France.

1724 Settlers establish Fort Dummer, Vermont first permanent white settlement.

1763 The Treaty of Paris ends the French and Indian War, and Vermont becomes English territory.

1775 Ethan Allen leads the Green Mountain Boys to capture New York's Fort Ticonderoga.

1777 Present-day Vermont declares itself an independent republic on January 15 and adopts its own constitution on July 8.

1785 Isaac Underhill opens the nation's first marble quarry in East Dorset.

1791 Vermont becomes the fourteenth state to join the United States on March 4.

1793 Vermont adopts its present constitution

1805 Montpelier becomes Vermont's capital city.

1823 The Champlain Canal opens, allowing for easier trade between Vermont and the rest of the United States.

United States History

The North and South fight **1861-65**
each other in the American Civil War.

The United States is **1917-18**
involved in World War I.

The stock market crashes, **1929**
plunging the United States into
the Great Depression.

The United States **1941-45**
fights in World War II.
The United States becomes a **1945**
charter member of the U.N.

The United States **1951-53**
fights in the Korean War.

The U.S. Congress enacts a series of **1964**
groundbreaking civil rights laws.

The United States **1964-73**
engages in the Vietnam War.

The United States and other **1991**
nations fight the brief
Persian Gulf War against Iraq.

Vermont State History

1859 Vermont's third and present capitol,
the State House, is built.

1881 Vermonter Chester A. Arthur assumes
the position of president of the United
States after James A. Garfield is
assassinated.

1911 Vermont's Bureau of Publicity becomes
the first tourism office in the United
States.

1923 Vermonter Calvin Coolidge becomes
president of the United States.
Vermont adopts its present state flag.

1927 The flooding of the Winooski River kills
sixty people in the state's worst natural
disaster.

1945 President Harry Truman chooses
Senator Warren R. Austin of Vermont
as the first U.S. ambassador to the
United Nations.

1974 Vermont elects Patrick Leahy, the
state's first Democratic senator since
the early 1800s.

1997 Legislature passes Act 60, a
constitutional school-funding law.

Fast Facts

State capitol

Statehood date	March 4, 1791, the 14th state
Origin of state name	From the French words *vert* (green) and *mont* (mountain). The Green Mountains were said to have been named by Samuel de Champlain. In 1777, Dr. Thomas Young suggested combining *vert* and *mont* into Vermont
State capital	Montpelier
State nickname	Green Mountain State
State motto	"Freedom and unity"
State bird	Hermit thrush
State animal	Morgan horse
State amphibian	Northern leopard frog

Monarch butterfly

Mount Mansfield

State flower	Red clover
State fishes	Brook trout and walleye
State insect	Honeybee
State butterfly	Monarch butterfly
State fossil	Charlotte, the whale fossil
State rocks	Granite, marble, and slate
State mineral	Talc
State gem	Grossular garnet
State song	"These Green Mountains"
State tree	Sugar maple
State fair	Rutland, early September
Total area; rank	9,615 sq. mi. (24,903 sq km); 43rd
Land; rank	9,249 sq. mi. (23,955 sq km); 43rd
Water; rank	366 sq. mi. (948 sq km); 44th
***Inland water;* rank**	366 sq. mi. (948 sq km); 40th
Geographic center	Washington, 3 miles (5 km) east of Roxbury
Latitude and longitude	Vermont is located approximately between 42° 44' and 45° 01' N and 71° 33' and 73° 26' W
Highest point	Mount Mansfield, 4,393 feet (1,340 m)
Lowest point	Lake Champlain in Franklin County, 95 feet (29 m) above sea level
Largest city	Burlington
Number of towns	246
Population; rank	564,964 (1990 census); 48th

Winter in Vermont

Density	59 persons per sq. mi. (23 per sq km)
Population distribution	28% urban, 72% rural

Ethnic distribution (does not equal 100%)

White	98.64%
Hispanic	0.65%
Asian and Pacific Islanders	0.57%
African-American	0.35%
Native American	0.30%
Other	0.14%

Record high temperature	105°F (41°C) at Vernon on July 4, 1911
Record low temperature	–50°F (–46°C) at Bloomfield on December 30,1933
Average July temperature	68°F (20°C)
Average January temperature	17°F (–8°C)
Average annual precipitation	39 inches (99 cm)

Natural Areas and Historic Sites

National Historical Park

Marsh-Billings National Historical Park preserves the home of George Perkins Marsh, pioneering conservationist.

National Scenic Trail

Appalachian National Scenic Trail is a 2,158-mile (3,472-km) trail extending the length of the Appalachian Mountains from Maine to Georgia.

Green Mountains

National Forests
Green Mountain National Forest preserves 345,000 acres (140,000 ha) in two sections of the Green Mountains.

State Parks
Vermont maintains approximately 90,000 acres (36,000 ha) in a number of state parks.

Sports Teams

NCAA Teams (Division 1)
University of Vermont Catamounts

Rokeby, a museum south of Burlington

Cultural Institutions

Libraries
The Bailey/Howe Library at the University of Vermont (Burlington) holds the state's largest book collection.

The Vermont State Library (Montpelier) and the *Vermont State Historical Society Library* (Montpelier) have fine collections on the state's history.

Museums
The Bennington Museum (Bennington) has collections featuring early American glassware, pottery, and flags.

The Sheldon Museum (Middlebury) houses early documents relating to Vermont's history, as well as portraits and household furnishings.

The Shelburne Museum (Shelburne) also contains objects relating to the state's history.

Performing Arts
Vermont has one major symphony orchestra.

University of Vermont

Universities and Colleges
In the late 1990s, Vermont had six public and sixteen private institutions of higher learning.

Annual Events

January–March
Town Meeting Day, throughout the state (first Tuesday in March)

April–June
The Annual Sugar Slalom in Stowe (April)

Vermont Maple Festival in St. Albans (April)

Vermont Dairy Festival in Enosburg Falls (June)

Antique Gas and Steam Engine Show in Brownington (June)

July–September
Old-Time Fiddlers Contest in Hardwick (July)

Vermont Quilt Festival in Northfield (July)

Arts Festival on the Green in Middlebury (July)

Vermont Mozart Festival in Burlington (July–August)

County Fairs in Barton, Bradford, Essex Junction, Lyndonville, Rutland, and Tunbridge (late August–September)

Foliage Festivals statewide (late September–October)

Calvin Coolidge

Famous People

Ethan Allen (1738–1789)	Painter
Chester Alan Arthur (1829–1886)	U.S. president
Calvin Coolidge (1872–1933)	U.S. president
John Deere (1804–1886)	Inventor and industrialist
George Dewey (1837–1917)	Naval officer

John Irving

John Dewey (1859–1952)	Philosopher, psychologist, and educator
Stephen Arnold Douglas (1813–1861)	Public official and political leader
James Fisk (1834–1872)	Financier
William Morris Hunt (1824–1879)	Artist
John Irving (1942–)	Writer
Bill Koch (1955–)	Skier
Joseph Smith (1805–1844)	Religious leader
Brigham Young (1801–1877)	Religious leader

To Find Out More

History

- Fradin, Dennis Brindell. *Vermont*. Chicago: Children's Press, 1993.

- Pelta, Kathy. *Vermont*. Minneapolis: Lerner, 1994.

- Thompson, Kathleen. *Vermont*. Austin, Tex.: Raintree/Steck Vaughn, 1996.

Biography

- Faber, Doris. *Robert Frost: America's Poet*. Englewood Cliffs, N.J.: Prentice-Hall, 1964.

- Nolan, Jeannette Covert. *The Little Giant: Stephen A. Douglas*. New York: J. Messner, 1964.

- Older, Jules. *Ben & Jerry — The Real Scoop!* Shelburne, Vt.: Chapters, 1993.

Fiction

- Fisher, Dorothy Canfield. *Understood Betsy*. Hanover, N.H.: University Press of New England, 1999.

- Hurwitz, Johanna. *Faraway Summer*. New York: William Morrow, 1998.

- Kinsey-Warnock, Natalie. *As Long As There Are Mountains*. New York: Cobblehill Books, 1997.

- Paterson, Katherine. *Jip: His Story*. New York: Lodestar Books, 1996.

- Peck, Robert Newton. *Hang for Treason*. Garden City, N.Y.: Doubleday, 1976.

- Wakefield, Pat A. *A Moose for Jessica*. New York: E. P. Dutton, 1987.

Websites

- **State of Vermont**
  http://www.cit.state.vt.us/
  The official website for the state of Vermont

- **Vermont Historical Society**
  http://www.cit.state.vt.us/vhs/
  For online exhibits, information about the society, and links

Addresses

- **Vermont Department of Travel and Tourism**
  134 State Street
  Montpelier, VT 05602
  For information about travel in Vermont

- **Agency of Development and Community Affairs**
  109 State Street
  Montpelier, VT 05602
  For information about Vermont's economy

- **Vermont Legislative Council**
  115 State Street
  Montpelier, VT 05602
  For information about Vermont's government

- **Vermont Historical Society**
  109 State Street
  Montpelier, VT 05602
  For information about Vermont's history

Index

Page numbers in *italics* indicate illustrations.

Meet the Author

Ann Heinrichs fell in love with faraway places while reading Doctor Dolittle books as a child. She has traveled through most of the United States and several countries in Europe, as well as north and west Africa, the Middle East, and east Asia.

Ann fell in love with Vermont the moment she heard the song "Moonlight in Vermont." When she finally got a chance to spend some leisure time there, she found the real Vermont was far lovelier than the song. "The air is full of woodsy smells, the streams are clear as rippling glass—and, yes, the moonlight on a crisp autumn evening is enchanting."

While her trips are fun, she says the real work—tracking down all the factual information for a book—begins at the library. "I head straight for the reference department. Some of my favorite resources are statistical abstracts and the library's computer databases.

"For this book, I also read local newspapers from several Vermont towns. The Internet was a super research tool, too. The state's home page on the World Wide Web and the state historical websites are chock full of information.

"For me, writing nonfiction is a more exciting challenge than writing fiction. With nonfiction, you can't just dream something up—everything has to be true. When I uncover the facts, they always turn out to be more spectacular than fiction could ever be."

Ann Heinrichs grew up in Fort Smith, Arkansas, and now lives in Chicago. She is the author of more than thirty-five books for children and young adults on American, Asian, and African history and culture. Several of her books have received state and national awards.

Ms. Heinrichs has also written numerous newspaper, magazine, and encyclopedia articles and critical reviews. As an advertising copywriter, she has covered everything from plumbing hardware to Oriental rugs, teddy bears, and porcelain dolls. She holds a bachelor's and master's degree in piano performance. These days, her performing arts are t'ai chi chuan and kung fu sword.

Photo Credits